# GENESIS &
# EVOLUTION

# GENESIS &
# EVOLUTION

## M.R.DEHAAN, M.D.

**ZONDERVAN
PUBLISHING HOUSE** OF THE ZONDERVAN CORPORATION
GRAND RAPIDS, MICHIGAN 49506

GENESIS AND EVOLUTION
Copyright 1962 by
Radio Bible Class
Grand Rapids, Michigan

Nineteenth printing  1981
ISBN 0-310-23361-5

Printed in the United States of America

# FOREWORD

It was my privilege to read the manuscript before this book was published. When I finished it, I said a hearty "Amen"! I immediately added this book as a "must" to the list of books which is required reading by our Word of Life staff members. We plan to use it at our camps, in our rallies, crusades and Bible clubs.

Thank God for such a defender of the faith as Dr. DeHaan who steadfastly sticks to the good "old paths" and "ancient landmarks" (Jeremiah 6:16 and 18:15). One does not have to look far to realize that we are living in the day which Paul spoke about in II Timothy 4:4, "And they shall turn away their ears from the truth, and shall be turned unto fables." When men deliberately turn their ears away from the truth, all they have left are the fables of this world. Praise the Lord, we can say with Peter, "We have not followed cunningly devised fables, when we made known unto you the power and coming of our Lord Jesus Christ" (II Peter 1:16).

I am sure your heart will be thrilled and challenged as you read this book.

— JACK WYRTZEN
*Word of Life Fellowship, Inc.*

# CONTENTS

# GENESIS &
# EVOLUTION

## Chapter One

## IN THE BEGINNING

*In the beginning God created the heaven and the earth (Genesis 1:1).*

This is God's first and final answer to the curiosity of man concerning the origin of the universe. Curiosity is as characteristic of man as the desire for food and drink. Curiosity is a thirst for knowledge, the desire to investigate, a yearning to know. This innate thirst for knowledge in itself is no sin, but it may assume two aspects. It is this thirst for "knowing," this desire to see and understand, which is at the basis of all progress and is the object of ceaseless research. The fact that man is not satisfied with what he knows, prompts him to investigate, search, analyze, experiment, and study to find out why and how things are. It is man's curiosity, his desire to know, which drives him on to dig into the earth, dive beneath the sea, and now causes him to invade outer space, in his yearning to open up new vistas of knowledge. It is curiosity which moves a person with overpowering desire to find out what is behind a closed door with a sign: "Keep Out." Why am I not allowed to see what is there? It is curiosity, a search for knowledge, which prompts the lad to take his father's watch apart, just to find out "what makes it tick." Every parent must prepare for the inevitable question of his inquisitive child, "Daddy, where did I come from?"

It is fear of the unknown which drives men in their curiosity to risk their lives in order to KNOW. An animal will often bring about its own destruction through curiosity. Upon seeing a strange object, it will approach with curiosity instead of fleeing before the unidentified enemy. Curiosity, therefore, may be a valuable asset in urging man onward in his pursuit of knowledge, or it may be the very trap in which he will destroy himself.

11

## THE APPEAL TO SIN

An illustration of this tragic result of misdirected curiosity is seen in the very dawn of human history. The fall of man was the direct result of curiosity. Satan knew the potentialities of man's desire for knowledge, and so approached the woman through the door of curiosity. He aroused her curiosity when he said, ". . . Yea, hath God said, Ye shall not eat of every tree of the garden?" (Genesis 3:1).

This was an appeal to Eve's curiosity. The question implied very subtly that there was something about that forbidden tree which Eve did not know. Why should God prohibit them from eating of that tree? What was there about this tree which necessitated the prohibition? It was a beautiful tree, pleasant to the eyes; it was a tree whose fruit was good and delicious (Genesis 3:6). Why then was it "taboo"? That was the question to which Eve wanted to know the answer. And Satan was right there, for he said: "For God doth know that in the day ye eat thereof, then your eyes shall be opened, and ye shall be as gods, *knowing* good and evil" (Genesis 3:5).

Notice the appeal of the serpent to Eve's curiosity — "your eyes shall be opened." "There are some things you don't see now. There are some things hidden behind that tree." And then "ye shall know." *Ye shall know!* It was her thirst for knowledge which caused her fall. It was her curiosity versus God's Word. Instead of believing God, she doubted, and allowed her curiosity to lead her to disobey God in an effort to prove that which must be accepted by faith. Instead of believing God's will, she seeks to test and prove it by her disobedience. Her curiosity led her to disobey the Word of God.

## HUMAN NATURE THE SAME

Now man has not changed one single whit since then. God has spoken, and expects man to believe it. We are to accept God's Word by faith. God is not obligated to explain the why and the how of His actions, but expects us to believe it. This is graphically illustrated in the very first sentence in the Word of

God: "In the beginning God created the heaven and the earth" (Genesis 1:1).

This can never be explained or understood by the creature; therefore, it must be accepted by faith. This is definitely clear from the book of Hebrews: "Through faith we understand that the worlds were framed by the word of God, so that things which are seen were not made of things which do appear" (Hebrews 11:3).

Man, however, wants evidence. He wants God to explain to his satisfaction just how He did it, and will not accept the simple final statement of Genesis 1:1. While this first verse in the Bible is God's final word on the origin of the universe, man's perverted curiosity is not satisfied with God's definitive statement, and so he seeks to invent his own idea for the origin of the universe, and comes up with a theory of evolution, which wholly or partially rules God out of His creation. Just as in the Garden of Eden, the question is still, "Will we believe God's Word or the speculations of science, so called?"

### ONE OR THE OTHER

We assert, therefore, that our attitude toward this opening statement of the Bible is the true test of faith in the rest of the Scriptures. The question therefore arises: Is this a literal account of the creation, or is it merely an allegory? Is this record of creation an actual statement of fact, or fiction and fable? This is the question upon which rest all other answers to the problem of death, sin, redemption, Heaven, and Hell. And right here the Bible and the modern theories of evolution come into direct conflict. Before contrasting evolution in general with the Bible account, we must first define evolution and distinguish between its various concepts. In its broadest meaning, evolution may be defined as an organic process of cumulative and genetic changes in the development of plants and animals. The earliest records of evolutionary studies date back to the Greeks in the days of Aristotle in the fourth century before Christ. He first taught that certain forms of life could be generated spontaneously, a theory totally abandoned by modern evolutionists who hold to the biogenetic reproduction of life.

## TWO KINDS OF EVOLUTION

In general, evolution is of two kinds: atheistic evolution and theistic evolution. Atheistic evolution would teach that either matter is eternal or that it was generated by inherent powers apart from a supreme intelligence or Creator. Theistic evolution, on the other hand, admits that there was an "Intelligence" which created the substance of the universe and guided it in its evolutionary development. This intelligence may be personal or impersonal. Theistic evolution can be even more dangerous than atheistic evolution because it does admit of a God of some sort. But when it proceeds to attribute to this God an evolutionary development whereby everything evolved from an original mass, a nebulous or primordial cell, and so that man came up through the lower animals until he evolved in the image of God, then theistic evolution is little better than atheistic evolution.

The Bible story of creation is so clear it admits of no evolution from a lower form to a higher. It says man was created (not evolved) by a separate act of God, and so stands above and apart from all the rest of creation. The Bible record of creation has stood the test of time, while the countless speculations, theories, and guesses of men are strewn, discarded and disproven, along the path of history. We have no quarrel with science — true science; we have no quarrel with evolution if by it we mean the improvement and development of plants and animals within the confines of Bible revelation. But much so-called science is not scientific, and wherever science and the Bible conflict, it is either because we have misinterpreted the Bible, or science was wrong and is still in error. There can be no conflict between *true* science and the *correct* interpretation of Scripture. God is the Author of *true* science, for science is the study of natural phenomena and the relations between them. Science deals with matter, the laws which govern it, and the phenomena it manifests; and since God is the Creator of matter and the Author of its laws and manifestations of its phenomena, God is the Author of true science. Basically nothing is truly scientific unless founded upon absolute fact. Unless substantiated by fact and proven to be a fact, it is only as Paul calls it "science . . . so called."

## BIBLE IS SCIENTIFIC

We repeat, there is no conflict — there can be no conflict between the correct interpretation of the Bible and true science. Any so-called interpretation of the Bible which is in conflict with an absolutely proven scientific fact, only proves that the interpretation was wrong, and the Bible meant quite another thing. In the same way any theory of science which is later disproved, brands it immediately as unscientific. And so we see that both science and theology suffer most at the hands of its own overenthusiastic, but incapable and amateur exponents. Sometimes science is correct and our interpretation of Scripture is wrong — and then again too often science is wrong because it rests on insufficient evidence.

Frequently we hear well-intentioned, sincere Bible students defend the apparent conflict between the Bible and science by the wholly false and erroneous statement, as follows: "Well, we must remember the Bible is not a scientific book. That is not its purpose. It was not intended to be scientific for it is a book of redemption, and not science. It deals with salvation and not the sciences, and so we must just ignore and overlook the unscientific statements in the Bible, and remember that if it is mistaken in its dealing with the matters of science, it is not a book of science, and we cannot expect it to be scientifically infallible." This is the biggest piece of nonsense ever attempted by well-meaning but shallow-thinking defenders of the Bible. Who is the Author of the Bible? Who is it that speaks with infallible authority in this Book? If this Book is not scientifically correct, then the Author of the Book was not scientific. God is the Author of the Bible. It is His revelation. In it He speaks with authority, infallible and unchangeable. It opens with: "In the beginning God created the heaven and the earth." And you say this Creator is not a scientist and doesn't understand natural phenomena, and must be excused for His ignorance in scientific matters? Think the statement through, my friend, when you hear someone say, sincerely trying to defend the Bible, "Well, we must remember the Bible is a book of redemption and not science, and we cannot expect it to be scientifically accurate." Think that statement through, and see the stupidity of such reasoning. Science is the knowledge of matter, natural phenomena, and the study of the physical universe. And He who made all these didn't know science? He who created the stars doesn't know astronomy, so what the Bible says about stars must be taken with a grain of salt? He who created matter out of nothing doesn't understand physics? He who created life, is ignorant of biology? He who made the elements is not an authority on chemistry? What foolish drivel is this! He who formed the earth doesn't know geology? He who meted out the heavens with a span is ignorant of geometry and astronomy, and He who created the atom which no one has ever seen, doesn't understand nuclear physics?

You see what a dangerous, vicious mistake it is to try to defend the Bible by saying it was not intended to be a book of science. To this statement we answer that God is the *only* infallible scientist, the Bible is the *only* book of absolute sciences, and wherever it deals with any branch of science: astronomy, physics, biology, chemistry, geology, mathematics, mechanics, or psychology, it speaks with the same infallible final authority. Not a single statement in the entire Bible has ever been disproven by *true* science, but in every case true science has confirmed the revelation of Scripture.

The Bible needs no such shallow defense. It can stand on its own feet. Since science deals with all the phenomena of nature and the universe, and God is the Creator of the universe, His statement sweeps all controversy before it by the simple statement with which we began: "In the beginning God created the heaven and the earth" (Genesis 1:1).

Once we believe that absolute statement, our faith comes to rest. We are not disturbed by the apparent conflict with so-called scientific discoveries, but are content to wait and see science finally come to agreement with the Word which is "forever settled in heaven." It becomes a matter of simple faith in God. And so the Bible opens with the message — "salvation by faith." The Bible is the book of redemption and salvation by "faith" in the Word of God. There is no other way of salvation than by believing God. No wonder then that the Bible opens with a statement which must be believed. It cannot be understood, explained, or proven — it must be accepted by faith. And what can be more reasonable? We put faith in men, who are fallible and often fail us. Why not put faith in the Word of God? In I John it is stated as follows:

> If we receive the witness of men, the witness of God is greater: for this is the witness of God which he hath testified of his Son.
> He that believeth on the Son of God hath the witness in himself: he that believeth not God hath made him a liar . . . (I John 5:9, 10).

There is no other way, for "he that cometh to God must *believe* that he is, and that he is a rewarder of them that diligently seek him" (Hebrews 11:6).

## Chapter Two

## GOD'S FIRST AND FINAL WORD

*In the beginning . . . (Genesis 1:1).*

IN THE BEGINNING! Thus does this marvelous, miraculous book, the Bible, open its wonderful revelation. In the beginning! The very first words of this book place the stamp of divine authorship upon it. It bears the indisputable evidence of its divine origin and inspiration. It begins with the bold, unapologetic assertion that "In the beginning God created." The first three words in our English Bible, "In the beginning," are only one word in the original. It is the Hebrew word, "bereshiyth." When, several centuries before Christ came, some seventy scholars translated the Hebrew Bible into Greek, the language of that day, they called this book *Genesis,* the Greek word for "beginning," a translation of the first word in the Bible.

No better name could possibly be given to the first book of the Bible, for it is indeed the book of beginnings. It is far more than a book which records the beginning, the origin, the creation of this earth on which we live and other heavenly bodies surrounding us in the universe. It records the beginning of all revelation. In this book we find not only the record of the beginning of the material creation, but also the revelation of the redemptive purpose of God in the new creation of salvation.

The book of Genesis has rightly been called the seed plot of Scripture. There is not a single doctrine, revelation or truth revealed in the rest of the sixty-five books of the Bible, which is not found in type or figure in the book of Genesis. The seed of every other revelation is here. In the book of Genesis, and particularly in the first three chapters, we have every Bible doctrine introduced, and the rest of the Scripture is but the unfolding of that which is already introduced in capsule form in the first three chapters of Genesis.

## MOST IMPORTANT VERSE

This being so — and we shall prove it — the first verse of the Bible becomes in a certain sense the most important verse in Scripture. The first verse of the Bible determines whether you are a believer or an infidel. What you think of this verse, "In the beginning God created the heaven and the earth," determines your whole attitude toward the rest of Scripture. If I can believe this simple statement, "In the beginning God created," I shall have no difficulty with the rest of Scripture. If God who always was, before the beginning, could create out of nothing but Himself, the whole universe, "the earth and the heavens," from the tiny atom to the greatest star — millions of light-years in space, then surely I will not doubt that a God who could do this by simply speaking one word, could also turn water into blood, part the Red Sea, rain manna from heaven, walk on the water, raise the dead, cast out demons, heal the sick, cleanse the lepers, make the sun stand still, and arise from the dead. But once you reject the first five words of Scripture, "In the beginning God created," (just three words in the original), once you reject these first three words, you cannot believe anything else in the Bible. How can we believe a book which begins with error?

## NO APOLOGIES

God makes no apologies for this statement — *In the beginning God created.* He does not stoop to explain *how* He did it, or even *why* He did. You either believe it or reject it. If you are wise, you will believe it; to reject it is to make a fool of yourself. This then is the starting point of faith — "In the beginning God." *In the beginning God.* Once you accept this, the rest is simple. All the monkey business of so-called science and anthropology, and all the other variant, changing guesses of men dissolve in the mists of mere human speculations. The theories of men concerning the origin of the universe, the theory of the primordial cell, the "vapor theory," and even theistic evolution, become so much foolishness when viewed in the light of this simple statement, "In the beginning God created." The fool rejects it; the wise man receives it.

## VOLUMES WRITTEN BY MAN

Man has tried to reconstruct the beginning of the universe, the earth, and his own origin by hundreds of theories and suppositions. He found a bone from an elephant, another from an ass, and a third from a monkey, and the skull of a man, and wiring them together, has constructed a museum specimen of a pre-historic man, and wants us to believe this was our grandfather.

## MAN'S GUESSES

Compare the simple record of the Bible, "In the beginning God created," (only three words in the original, *bereshiyth bara elohim*) with the speculations of so-called science, and I appeal to your common sense and reason, which is the most credible and logical? Evolution tells us that in the beginning there was a nebulous mass or a primordial cell. Fine! This is the explanation man gives. In the beginning a "cell" — *a single cell*. This cell divided and there were two cells; they divided and there were four; then eight, then sixteen, then thirty-two, then sixty-four, and then the sixty-four organized and developed special functions and — ! Sounds simple, doesn't it? — Now wait a minute! Wait a minute! Hold everything! Before you go any further with your presumptive first premise, let's start over. Let's go back a bit. Tell me, where did this first cell come from? Who made that first cell? "Well," you say, "it always was!" Indeed! Isn't that interesting! A primitive cell always was — an unintelligent, brainless cell was the beginning of everything.

Compare with this the first four words of Scripture, "In the beginning God," *God*, GOD — an infinite, all-wise, all-powerful God, *created*. The evolutionist says in the beginning a single cell — a brainless cell. The choice is between a simple, unintelligent little glob of protoplasm, and an omnipotent, omniscient, eternal, beginningless God. Take your choice. I do declare, it is ten thousand times easier for me to believe: "In the beginning God" than: "In the beginning a blob of impersonal, unintelligent protoplasm." Surely the *fool* has said in his heart, "There is no God" (Psalm 14:1).

## NO SALVATION WITHOUT GOD

You see then how important the first verse of the Bible becomes. Salvation depends not only on John 3:16 or Romans 10:13 or Acts 16:31; it depends primarily on whether you believe Genesis 1:1, "In the beginning God created." We must begin at the beginning. If you reject this, you cannot believe anything else in the Bible. If Genesis 1:1 is not true, the Bible is a lie, for it begins with a "lie." Reject Genesis 1:1, and you call God a "liar." That's a pretty serious charge, you say. I know it is, for it involves Heaven or Hell for you. That is why I am emphasizing this first verse. On it depends your eternal destiny and salvation. The writer of Hebrews said: "But without faith it is impossible to please him: for he that cometh to God must believe that he *is*, and that he is a rewarder of them that diligently seek him" (Hebrews 11:6).

You must "believe" what God says, and what God says begins in Genesis 1:1, "In the beginning God created." Jesus said: "And this is life eternal, that they might know thee the only true God, and Jesus Christ, whom thou hast sent" (John 17:3).

In the beginning God! No other book could open with that statement, except the Bible. The only one who can tell us about the beginning must be the One who was there. That is why man cannot start at the beginning and move forward, but he starts with the end and tries to work backward. And in this search for the beginning of things, the scientists found many evidences of evolution, progress, and development, but never came to the beginning of it all — "In the beginning God." And this God, when He created the inhabitants of this earth, created them in separate, distinct acts on successive days. On the third day He created vegetation — herbs, trees, and grass. If God followed the pattern of evolution, the appearance of animal life would have evolved without a break, and it should appear on the next day, the fourth. But not so. Between the appearance of vegetation on the third day and the coming of animal life on the fifth day, a whole day lies between — the fourth day, in which God *did nothing on this earth*. There was a lull in the series of replenishing the earth, and God is occupied with the heavenly bodies, the sun, moon, and stars (Genesis 1:14-19). And after this pause of one whole day — separating the plant life from animal life — God resumed the work of re-populating the sea and earth with fish and fowl. Why this one whole day between the vegetable realm and the animal? We sincerely believe it was to emphasize the fact that animal life did not evolve from the vegetable. There was no gradual evolution of plant into fish and fish into fowl and fowl into ape and ape into man.

## FORM OF EVOLUTION

There is, of course, evolution and change within the various species of plants and animals, but never a crossing over from one into the other — never a gradual process by which a plant became a fish or a fowl. This is the error which modern man makes. He recognizes the fact that the effect of climate, food, environment, and natural enemies have caused great changes in plants and animals, resulting in diversities so great that they have lost much of their resemblance to one another, but one species never evolves into another.

Just an example: There are many different kinds of oak trees in the world — all the offspring of a single acorn — a single seed. Through generations of change they have evolved or degenerated into various kinds or varieties. Depending on soil and minerals, rainfall, heat, and climate, they have by inherent, divinely created natural powers adapted themselves to these varying environments so that some acorns are huge in size, and in other areas small. Some are light brown, others dark; thick-shelled and thin-shelled; sweet or bitter. Almost limitless are the changes which may occur due to different conditions. But they are all *oak trees* bearing only acorns. Think of the varieties of apples produced by cultivation, careful selective pollination and crossing, but man still has not been able to grow an orange on an apple tree. All these changes and adaptations occur only within the limits of the species. And this the Word of God asserts in Genesis 1, that He made the fruit tree yielding its fruit after its kind (species), the birds after their kind, and the various animals after their kind. And the missing link between the species has never been found, for it does not exist. More on this later.

As we close the chapter, we must apply this to the matter of redemption. Adam brought forth children after his kind — natural children — sinners by birth. This old nature, the Adamic nature, is transmitted to the whole race "after its kind." We may cultivate it, educate it, refine it, seek to improve it, but it will never evolve into a saint. In whatever form it appears, it is still the old Adamic nature. Jesus said, "That which is born of the flesh is flesh" (John 3:6). He only enunciated the divine principle laid down in Genesis 1, "Let it bring forth after its kind." A cat never has puppies, a horse never has a calf, chicken eggs never hatch ducklings, and pigs never bare lambs; and flesh never becomes spirit, and the old Adam never becomes a new man. And that is why we must be born again, born from above. There is no evolution of a sinner into a saint, any more than there is evolution of a monkey into a man. "Ye must be born again." This is the Word of God. Whom will you believe, God or man? Jesus said:

> He that believeth on him is not condemned: but he that believeth not is condemned already, because he hath not believed on the name of the only begotten Son of God (John 3:18).

*Chapter Three*

# THE AUTHOR OF SIN

*In the beginning God created the heaven and the earth (Genesis 1:1).*

*Therefore if any man be in Christ, he is a new creature: old things are passed away; behold, all things are become new (II Corinthians 5:17).*

*In the beginning God created.* Thus the Bible account of creation opens and begins its revelation of God's great plan of salvation. Salvation is of the Lord, and hence the Bible begins with the great source of all creation, both the old and the new, both the material and the spiritual re-creation. No argument is presented for the existence of God. No statement is given as to where He came from. He is the great I AM, the One "that is and was and is to come." God lives in the eternal present. He has no past and no future, but lives in the eternal present, "I AM." This first verse of the Bible is the terse and absolute record of God, concerning the creation of the universe. No details are added, no explanation is given. You are expected to believe it because God says it. God, the Creator, is not obligated to tell His puny creature man any more than He is pleased to tell. Hence God says, and here is the statement: "In the beginning God created the heaven and the earth." You may believe it or reject it, but only upon pain of eternal consequences.

## A PERFECT CREATION

Now this original creation of God described in the first verse of the Bible was a *perfect* creation. Everything that God made was *very good*. We shall presently show that God's original creation was not like the next verse describes it, as waste "without

24

form, and void." Everything God made was good and perfect. The creation of Genesis 1:1 was flawlessly perfect. But in the very next verse (Genesis 1:2) we find a ruined creation, in chaos and disorder as the result of some great cataclysmic catastrophe. It is described as follows: "And the earth was without form, and void; and darkness was upon the face of the deep . . ." (Genesis 1:2).

It has been pointed out that the words, "was without form," should be translated "*became* without form, and void." It was not thus in the beginning. God never made anything waste or void. That is the result of sin. We read in Isaiah: ". . . God himself that formed the earth and made it; he hath established it, he created it not in vain, he formed it to be inhabited . . ." (Isaiah 45:18).

The word "vain" in this verse is "*tohuw*" (pronounced tohoo) and means "waste." Here is God's word, that in the beginning He did not make the earth waste as in Genesis 1:2. The verse in Isaiah 45 refers to the original creation as recorded in the first verse of Genesis 1. But the second verse records the earth as it was *after* something had happened to plunge the earth into darkness and make it waste and void. Now there is only one thing that could bring the earth under the curse, and that one thing is sin. So, somewhere in the period between the first and second verses of Genesis, sin entered with its resultant curse and the description found in verse 2. This sin could have had but one source. God could not sin. Man was not yet created, and the only other creatures existent before the creation of man were the angels. And it was among these angels, under the leadership of Lucifer, the Shining One, an archangel of great power and beauty, that a rebellion took place against God, and Lucifer fell; his angels became demons and the earth was placed under the curse. We have the record of this fall graphically given in Isaiah 14:

> How art thou fallen from heaven, O Lucifer, son of the morning! how art thou cut down to the ground, which didst weaken the nations!
> For thou hast said in thine heart, I will ascend into heaven, I will exalt my throne above the stars of God:

I will sit also upon the mount of the congregation, in the
sides of the north:
I will ascend above the heights of the clouds; I will
be like the most High.
Yet thou shalt be brought down to hell, to the sides
of the pit.
They that see thee shall narrowly look upon thee, and
consider thee, saying, Is this the man that made the earth
to tremble, that did shake kingdoms;
That made the world as a wilderness, and destroyed
the cities thereof; that opened not the house of his
prisoners? (Isaiah 14:12-17).

There is every scientific evidence of a prehistoric creation on
this earth. Geologic examination of the earth's surface reveals
that in the dim distant past there flourished on this earth a vegetation of unusual luxuriance, and prehistoric animals of gigantic
size, distinctly separate and different in character from anything
we know now. We find fossils of these prehistoric animals which
lived millions of years ago. In our coal deposits we find the evidence of luxuriant tropical vegetation. Oil is known to be the
result of decomposed animal and vegetable matter dating back
millions of years, so that the slogan of one oil company, "mel-
lowed ninety-nine million years" may not be far amiss. All scientific evidence points to this prehistoric period, with its primitive
animal life, vegetation, and spirit civilization. Not many years
ago these findings were rejected by orthodox theologians until
it was pointed out that the first and second verses of Genesis 1
do not describe the same period. In Genesis 1:1 we have the
creation as it came from the hand of God, perfect and abound-
ing in a beautiful and gorgeous, as well as gigantic, creation of
animals and vegetation. On this prehistoric earth Lucifer the
Archangel was placed, and his abode was EDEN according to
Ezekiel 28:13,

Thou hast been in Eden the garden of God; every
precious stone was thy covering . . . in the day that
thou wast created.
Thou art the anointed cherub that covereth; and I
have set thee so: thou wast upon the holy mountain of
God . . . .
Thou wast perfect in thy ways from the day that thou
wast created, till iniquity was found in thee (Ezekiel
28:13-15).

That is the record God gives of Lucifer. God placed him in Eden, the prehistoric Eden which geology has now uncovered. Then he sinned and fell. He was banished from the earth and cast out of Heaven and consigned to the atmosphere between Heaven and earth and thus has become the "prince of the power of the air." He has access to Heaven under limitations and also to the earth, but his abode is the "atmosphere above the earth."

## THE EARTH CURSED

As a result of his fall after his dominion on the prehistoric earth (we do not know how long he dwelt here) God cast him out and cursed the earth, and we find it as it became in verse 2 of Genesis 1: ". . . without form, and void; and darkness was upon the face of the deep. . . ."

How long the earth lay thus without form and void and under darkness we do not know. It may well be countless millions of years while the coal and oil deposits slowly formed. A study of the earth's crust reveals the various strata which tell of a great cataclysmic convolution of the earth in the dateless past. So you see again that the Bible record and the findings of *true* science always agree. Study that second verse of Genesis 1 carefully and you will detect in this brief statement a picture of an awful curse. It was without form; that is, it had no purpose. It was void, which means waste and useless. It was in darkness; that means that God had withdrawn Himself, for God is light; and where darkness is, it indicates the absence of God. It was covered by water, even as science agrees the earth was at one time.

## THE GREAT ICE AGE

Here in this verse, too, is the reference to the great ice age of which science tells. Science informs us that once the whole earth was covered with a great glacier or sheet of ice, which moved steadily down, gouging out the oceans and valleys and piling up the great mountains. Well, the Bible throws light on this assertion. In Genesis 1:1 there is no mention of seas. But in Genesis 1:2 it tells us that the earth was covered with water. Since there was no light, and the sun had not yet been set for a light of the day, there was no heat. Hence the waters in Genesis

1:2 *must* have been frozen just exactly as science now claims, but it was already revealed in the opening statement of Genesis. Under this darkness and this curse the earth lay for an undetermined period of time. And then God began a *new creation*.

## THE RE-CREATION

After this period of darkness and icy death God begins to work. Notice it was not the earth that began to awaken and by residential forces come to life. It did not begin to evolve out of its frozen state, but it began with God, for we read: ". . . And the Spirit of God moved [brooded] upon the face of the waters" (Genesis 1:2).

The Spirit of God who is *light* and *warmth* began to brood upon the icy wastes. The word "moved" means to "brood," like a bird upon its eggs. It means to impart warmth. The ice began to melt. How long this brooding period lasted is again immaterial, but after a longer or shorter period God spoke the word and the darkness disappeared and *light came*. God was again in His creation. The one great requisite for life, *light,* was again present. This was the first day of the *new* creation. Then follow the other six days in their logical order as God rehabilitates the earth and makes it ready for the occupation of another order of beings to be created in the very image of God. It is significant that while science finds incontestable evidence of an animal and vegetation creation dating back millions of years, no conclusive evidence of the presence of man farther back than six thousand years has ever yet been produced. They have speculated and brought together some bones and called it the "Neanderthal Man" or something else, but it is all in the field of imagination, speculation, and guess work.

## EVOLUTION

Evolutionists tell us with a great deal of boasting that they have now discovered how the earth evolved. They say it came like this: First there was a watery waste. Then land appeared as the earth cooled off. Then primitive plant life appeared out of the waters. Then the trees came and after that the birds, fish, and reptiles, and finally the mammals and man. Well, they did not have to discover that. They could have read it all in the first chapter of the Bible. Only here it is not evolution, but by the intelligent creation of Almighty God. However, the order is the same. Notice the seven days of creation as given by Moses four thousand years ago, and it makes science seem just a little late in its so-called discovery. Here are the days:

1. First day — *light*
2. Second day — *separation of vapors*
3. Third day — *plant life*
4. Fourth day — *sun, moon, stars*
5. Fifth day — *birds and fish*
6. Sixth day — *mammals and man*
7. Seventh day — *completed work*

This too may solve the problem which has been such a theme for discussion among both scientists and theologians. Did the earth come into being in seven successive ages of indefinite duration, or were the days of creation actual days of twenty-four literal hours each? That the seven days in Genesis 1 were of twenty-four hours each cannot be doubted. But there is nothing to indicate that the original creation of Genesis 1:1 may not have covered countless ages. God is the timeless One and time means nothing to Him. So gather up the picture. In the beginning God created a perfect earth. Over this earth Lucifer, the Shining One, had dominion. But he fell and rebelled against God and was cast out of the earth as his home. The earth became waste and void through sin, and then God begins His work of re-creation and completes it in seven literal days.

## THE SPIRITUAL CREATION

Now all of this is introductory to the real purpose for which this record is given. It is not primarily to satisfy our curiosity concerning our origin, but to acquaint us with the plan of salvation and our destiny. The story of creation is a parable of the plan of salvation. Man, too, like the material creation, was made good and perfect, in God's own image. But sin came again and caused man to fall and come under the curse of God. He was plunged in spiritual darkness and came under the icy deluge of God's judgment. That is where God finds the sinner and begins

His redemptive work with the brooding, convicting power of the Holy Spirit as in Genesis 1:3, and after a shorter or longer period God says, "Let there be light," and conversion follows. The darkness is gone and the light of God's Word brings the light of salvation. This is conversion, when the sinner hears the Word and responds to it. And then there follow six more days of replenishing, growth in grace and knowledge, till it is completed in the perfect rest of the seventh day.

The story of creation is a parable of the New Creation. Paul says: "Therefore if any man be in Christ, he is a *new creation*" (II Corinthians 5:17). It all begins with God, and comes only by His Word.

## Chapter Four

## GOD'S RE-CREATION

*In the beginning God created the heaven and the earth.*

*And the earth was without form, and void; and darkness was upon the face of the deep. And the Spirit of God moved upon the face of the waters.*

*And God said, Let there be light: and there was light.*

*And God saw the light, that it was good: and God divided the light from the darkness.*

*And God called the light Day, and the darkness he called Night. And the evening and the morning were the first day (Genesis 1:1-5).*

*Therefore if any man be in Christ, he is a new creature: old things are passed away; behold, all things are become new (II Corinthians 5:17).*

God is far more interested in the future of man than He is in his past; in his destiny than in his origin and history. It is for this reason that only one verse in the Bible is devoted to the record of the origin of the universe and that verse is Genesis 1:1, "In the beginning God created the heaven and the earth." God devotes only one chapter to the interesting record of how He clothed this earth with plants and animals and made man in His own image. This is found in chapter two of Genesis. Only one chapter is devoted to recounting the details of man's fall in the Garden of Eden. This is in chapter three. All the rest of the Bible, the balance of Genesis and all of the other sixty-five books, deal with man's salvation and his destiny. The very structure of Scripture and the proportion of space given to man's origin and his destiny indicates that God is far more interested in man's future than in his miserable and ignominious past.

## SIN PERVERTED MAN

But foolish man has reversed this order. Sin has so twisted human nature and perverted his thinking that instead of being interested in his future, he seems to be occupied with only one thing, namely, "Where did I come from?" And so he digs in the earth and reconstructs fossils, and delves into geology in an effort to find when and how the earth evolved and whether man evolved from a tree-climbing ape or an anthropoid monkey. How foolish indeed! The past is gone! The record is not a pleasant one, and the deeper we delve, the more sordid the story becomes. But this is not the worst of it. While so deeply engrossed in his past, man utterly neglects his future. Man by nature is not interested in where he is going, which after all is of far greater importance than from where he came. There is an interminable eternity ahead and man's place in that eternity is determined by what he does with God's plan of salvation now. So depraved is human nature by sin that man refuses to concern himself with his all-important future and is engrossed only with the irrelevant past. However, in Scripture we find that God dismisses the question of man's origin in one or two chapters and devotes the rest of His revelation to his destiny. He who is wise will do the same; and he who neglects to do so, is of all men the greatest fool.

## PLAN OF SALVATION

We have, therefore, in the first chapter of Genesis not only the record of the original material creation, its ruin, and its re-creation, but also a picture of the plan of salvation. We find the universe coming perfect from the hand of God in Genesis 1:1. It is ruined by Satan and sin, and results in the picture of destruction in Genesis 1:2. Then God begins to re-create by the brooding of the Spirit of God and the creation of light, the one essential for all organic life, in verse three. So too God made man good in His image, in the beginning. Sin came again through Satan and man was ruined, cursed, and lost. That is where God finds the sinner. Then begins the work of salvation, and this is called significantly enough by Paul: a *new creation*. "Therefore if any man be in Christ, he is a *new creation*." The word "creature" in II Corinthians 5:17 is literally "creation."

Thus God refers us back to *creation* when speaking of what we are *in Christ*.

Because the story of this earth's creation is a picture of the spiritual new creation, it is of utmost importance what view we take in this original record of creation in Genesis 1 to 3. If the first three chapters of the Bible are merely a parable, or symbolism, a fable, an allegory, or a myth, then the rest of the revelation of Scripture must also be accepted as a fable, an allegory, or a symbol. If the record of the material creation is not literal, how can we accept the new creation as literal? We therefore insist that Genesis 1 to 3 is a literal account of the creation of the world, its inhabitants, and man. It is a literal account of how sin and death and sorrow entered the race. It is a literal account of the strategies of Satan, of the curse of God on creation, and a literal account of God's plan of redemption in the slaying of a substitute to atone for man's sin (Genesis 3:21). To deny the literal account of creation is to destroy the reality of sin, and death, and sorrow. If the record of Genesis 3 is not literally true, then what explanation can we give for the fact of sin, disease, violence, death, destruction, and war? Then how can we account for the depravity of human nature? Then how do we know the records of the Gospel to be literally true?

## DESTROYS THE CROSS

However, the situation is even more serious. If we get rid of the literal account of the fall of man, and God's curse on creation, and His redemption by the shedding of the blood of an animal to provide the skins for man's covering, then the necessity of the Cross is destroyed. Then the whole plan of salvation becomes a myth, with no more credence than the mythological Pandora's Box. If the first three chapters of Genesis are not a literal account, then let us throw the Bible away and be done forever with the idle superstition and a senseless fetish of faith in a book which is only a collection of ancient fables.

## THE SCIENTIFIC BOOK

Instead of being what infidels consider it to be, however, the Bible is the most scientific book of facts the world has ever known. Though some of it was written over four thousand years ago, and the rest of it nearly two thousand years ago, there is not one statement which subsequent discoveries and progress have found to be untrue. Whether the Bible speaks on the subject of sin and redemption, anatomy, biology, physics, physiology, astronomy, chemistry, mathematics, or geology, its statements have stood for these thousands of years, and have been proven absolutely scientific and one hundred percent factual. The world's scientific works are outdated in a few brief years, but the Bible defies every attack, according to its own testimony. "For ever, O Lord, thy word is settled in heaven" (Psalm 119:89).

Or as Peter tells us: "But the word of the Lord endureth for ever . . ." (I Peter 1:25).

## THE SEVEN DAYS

The test of this indestructibility of the Word of God is found in Genesis 1. With the first three chapters of the Bible the entire Book stands or falls. Moses wrote some four thousand years ago the account of the creation. After the original creation was destroyed and cursed by Satan's sin, God began to re-create the earth for the occupation of man in His own image. This re-creation was done in the seven days of creation as given in chapter one of Genesis. They were as follows:

1. The first day—*Light*
2. The second day—*Dividing the Waters*
3. The third day—*Vegetation Created*
4. The fourth day—*Heavenly Bodies Made Visible*
5. The fifth day—*Fish and Birds*
6. The sixth day—*Cattle and Man*
7. The seventh day—*Rest*

Can you imagine Moses living four millenniums ago recounting this perfect, logical order of things unless divinely instructed? Moses was not there when God created light, fish and fowl, beasts and man. Even Adam was not there. How then did Moses know about all this? He was not present. There is only one answer—divine revelation. The lame and silly explanation that this record of creation was handed down by tradition from Adam to Moses reveals an utter lack of sense. It is claimed that because of the longevity of the antediluvians, the traditions were handed down from father to son, before there was any written record. If these traditions were handed down for two thousand years, how do we then explain the accuracy of Moses' account? How can one account for the fact that there was no distortion in the handing down of the record from one to another, and that the record is infallibly scientific and true?

Suppose it were handed down by tradition — then where did the tradition start? With whom did it begin? Suppose it began with father Adam—then where did Adam get the information? He was not created until after all the rest was made. Since Adam did not appear until all the events of Genesis 1 were finished, then Adam must have received his information by divine revelation. And if God could give it to Adam by revelation, it was no harder for Him to give it to Moses in the same way. How silly, how inane, how utterly stupid, the attempts of man to discredit the Word of God!

## GOD SPOKE THE WORD

The record of Genesis is therefore the literal record which God gave by infallible inspiration. The Bible claims this for itself. God spake unto Moses (Exodus 6:2, 6:13, 12:1, 16:11, 25:1, etc., etc., etc.). In Exodus 20:1 we read: "And God spake all these words, saying, I am the LORD thy God, which have brought thee out of the land of Egypt, out of the house of bondage" (Exodus 20:1, 2).

The Bible, therefore, is the Word of God, and the record of the seven days of creation could only be by the revelation of God, for there was no man present to witness it. Someone has said, "God made man last of all, lest he should interfere with God's perfect work."

Once again, before leaving the discussion of the material creation, we remind you that all these things were written for a far more important reason than just to explain the origin of the earth. They were written to illustrate God's great plan of salvation. The record of Creation is a picture of the new creation, and Paul calls the believer "a new creation." The parallel between the creation in Genesis 1 and the new creation in

Christ Jesus is so striking that one cannot miss the application. It begins with man created in God's image, but ruined by the fall. Then God begins to work, "for salvation is of the Lord." The first thing is the brooding of the Spirit upon the heart of the sinner, and with its melting, convicting power preparing him for the first initial step in salvation. This is conversion, and it corresponds to the first day of creation.

## LET THERE BE LIGHT

This is followed by the second day when God separated the *earthly waters* from the *heavenly*. The believer now is to live a life of separation from the world, and seek those things which are above where Christ is. Then comes the third day—when vegetation and fruit appears. This speaks of soul winning, as the fruit of the believer. Having been saved, and separated, we must now become fruitful, and this is followed by the fourth day—the setting of the lights of the sun, moon, and stars in heaven. It speaks of testimony—letting our light shine before men. This is followed by day number five, when God made birds to fly in the air and fish to swim in the sea. These speak of victory. A bird defies the forces of gravity, and mounts into the sky on its wings. A fish can survive in the dark waters of the ocean; it speaks of overcoming obstacles which bind us down to earth. It is Christian victory.

The sixth day speaks of service, labor and work. The cattle were beasts of burden. They were created on the sixth day. It speaks of production, labor, and fruitful endeavor, ending with the completion of the image of God in man. The seventh day, that of rest and peace, speaks of the goal and aim of the believer begun on that first day, when God said, "Let there be light."

This is the story of the *new creation*. How far have you advanced? Have you been enlightened by God's Spirit and been saved? Have you made any progress since then? Are you living a separated life? Is there fruit in your life? Does your testimony shine for Christ? Do you know anything about victory? Are you serving Him each day, and do you know the "peace of God which passeth all understanding"? How far have you gone in your Christian life? Where and why did you stop in your Christian growth? May God help you to check on your *new creation*.

## Chapter Five

## SCIENCE AND THE BIBLE

*In the beginning God created the heaven and the earth* (Genesis 1:1).

*In the beginning! In the beginning God!* Unsurpassed, indescribable, incomparable, for sheer majesty, grandeur and sublimity, is this opening statement of the Word of the Lord. Stamped indelibly upon it is the voice of finality, authority, sovereignty, and power. "In the beginning God." These words are not only the *first word* of God to man concerning his origin, but it is at the same time also the *last* word. There is no more to be said. In the beginning God! Man may try to substitute philosophy, science, evolution, for the Word of God, but God's first statement still stands as the *last* word concerning the origin and creation of this earth. It answers every question with finality and authority. And this statement has stood the test of time, often challenged but never answered, often disputed but never refuted, often reviled but never revised, often denounced but never destroyed.

### KEY TO WHOLE BIBLE

These first words of God's written revelation, "In the beginning God," are not only the introduction to the Bible, but are the Bible in germ form, God's revelation in nuclear state. What is true of the first verse in Genesis is true of the rest of the Scriptures. On this opening verse depends everything which follows. If this is not true, then all the rest falls with it. It may therefore well be called the most important verse in Scripture, for upon its acceptance or rejection all else rests. Here infidelity begins; here faith comes to rest. Believe this first verse and we will have no difficulty believing aught else in the Scriptures.

37

Reject this first phrase of Scripture and we cannot believe anything else in a book which begins with a lie. If this verse is not true, the whole book is unreliable, for the Bible claims for itself to be the infallible revelation of truth. David says: "For ever, O LORD, thy word is settled in heaven" (Psalm 119:89).

The Bible, the infallible Word of God, is therefore a unique and miraculous Book which, while written millenniums ago, has needed no revision or change or alteration. It is unique in its beginning. It is unique in its claims of authority. It declares its truths are settled in Heaven because its author is God. The Bible is unique in its character. It claims for itself that it is infallible and absolutely the last word on any subject with which it deals. The Bible is unique in its content, for it deals with every subject under heaven, and is the final authority on every subject with which it deals. This makes the Bible the most scientific Book under heaven. When the Bible speaks about science, geography, history, geology, chemistry, hygiene, sanitation, medicine, astronomy, physics, physiology, or mathematics, it speaks with the same infallible authority as when it speaks of spiritual matters and salvation. This is a proven fact, overlooked by the average student of the Scriptures.

Well-meaning but ill-informed, would-be defenders of the Bible try to excuse the apparent conflict of the Bible with the findings of so-called modern science by saying the Bible is not supposed to be a scientific book, and does not claim to be an authority on matters scientific, but is a book of salvation. They say we must therefore overlook its errors in matters scientific. No more baseless and damaging statement could be made. The Bible is just as infallible in one matter as another with which it deals. Since science deals with matter and things created, who could possibly be a greater authority on such matters than the Creator Himself?

## IN THE BEGINNING

The proof of this statement lies in the unique and supernatural way in which the Bible introduces itself: "In the beginning God created the heaven and the earth" (Genesis 1:1).

In the beginning! When the universe *began,* God was already

there. He made it all, created it out of *nothing*, and He is therefore the final and absolute authority on all things in creation,
whether it deals with history, geology, anthropology, astronomy,
and all other sciences.

## THE PENTATEUCH

The first five books of Moses are some four thousand years
old. Yet they are as scientific and up-to-date as any book written
in the twentieth century. After billions of years since the earth
was created, the man Moses described this original creation
and said: "In the beginning God created the heaven and the
earth" (Genesis 1:1).

He wrote this four millenniums ago and a better explanation
has never been successfully attempted. It is still the most reasonable, logical explanation of the question: "Where did we
come from?"

Once upon a time there was no time. There was no creation.
From a beginningless eternity, God was all alone in that perfect
family love-life of Father, Son, and Holy Ghost. There in that
eternity He counseled with Himself and planned to make a
creation and a universe. But He had *nothing* to begin with but
Himself. Yet at the proper moment He spake and creation began, for "In the beginning God created the heaven and the
earth." When the time came for the creative act, He reached
down the hand of His omnipotence into the great abyss of infinite emptiness and threw it out into nowhere, and "nothing
became *something*"; and from His Almighty fingers there
streamed forth the universe with its planets and suns, its sys-
tems and constellations and endless galaxies, as He sent them
forth, calling each one by its name while He hung them in the
chandeliers of heaven, garnished them with stardust and made
them dance to the music of the spheres. If I can believe this,
then I can believe that God could make a fish that could
swallow a man, that Christ could walk on the water, that God
could make the sun and the moon obey His command and
lengthen Joshua's day. Then I can believe that He could part
the Red Sea and make the Jordan stand on its feet. Then I
can believe that He could turn water into blood and rain fire

from heaven. Then I can believe that He could make an ass to speak, and rain bread from heaven for the children of Israel. It all depends on whether you believe: *In the beginning God.*

This is the answer to all speculations and guesses. Compare with this the theorizing of man. Listen to man as he tells us that in the beginning there was a primordial cell or a great super-heated nebula and as it cooled it formed a semi-solid mass of matter. By its rapid revolutions, masses flew off from the mother mass and formed suns and worlds and other planets. Some cooled off and became inhabited. Others remained hot and became stars and suns. Then the one we call the earth became covered with slime, and some of the slime began to crawl, and finally developed fins and became a fish. The fish changed its fins for feet and became a reptile. The reptile grew hair and a tail and became a monkey, and the monkey caught its tail in a crotch of the tree, fell down to earth and suddenly awoke to find that he was your great great-grandfather. That is the theory man would have us believe. But the Bible says, "God created man in His own image." I ask you in all seriousness, What is the more reasonable explanation of the origin of this creation, this theory of man, or the simple *in the beginning God created?*

*In the beginning God.* The Bible offers no proof for the existence of God except the universe itself which He created. You are expected to believe it. All evidence supports it. Even the heathen in darkest savagery believes in a God, whatever form that God may take. It waited for civilized man to invent the inane and insane theory of atheism. Even the inanimate creation extols and acknowledges its Creator: "The heavens declare the glory of God; and the firmament sheweth his handywork" (Psalm 19:1).

The hills are said to skip like lambs at His approach, and all the trees of the field clap their hands in glee at the mention of His name. Of all earth's creatures only man rebels against God and says in his heart, "There is no God."

## POINT OF ATTACK

Whether man knows the importance of the opening record of Scripture or not, there can be no question about the Devil's respect for the strategic importance of the first verse of Scripture (Genesis 1:1), as may be seen by his relentless attack upon this part of the Word of God. No portion of the Bible is more persistently and viciously attacked than the five books of Moses, and particularly the record of creation in the first three chapters of Genesis. Just disprove the first verse, and all the rest falls with it. The theories of evolution are shamelessly presented as a flat contradiction of the literal record of the creation of man in the image of God, and are aimed at disproving the opening verse of Scripture. The reason for the attack on the writings of Moses and especially his record of creation is easy to understand. If we can repudiate or disprove the authenticity of the Pentateuch we have destroyed the very foundation on which all of Scripture rests. But there is even a more serious implication, a clever, subtle attack upon the *authority* not only of Moses, but upon the *authority* and *truthfulness* of Jesus Christ. Prove that Moses did *not* write the books of the Pentateuch and you prove that Jesus was totally mistaken and not the infallible Son of God He claimed to be. Upon your faith in Moses as the writer of the five books attributed to him rests also your faith in Jesus as the Son of God. You cannot believe in Jesus Christ without believing what Moses wrote. You see, there is much more involved in denying the books of Moses than most people suppose.

If this seems like an extreme statement, consider these words of Jesus, for Jesus quoted more frequently from the writings of Moses than any other part of the Old Testament. Jesus believed, taught, and asserted that the books of Moses were authentic, binding, and as genuine as He Himself. Listen to Jesus in Mark 12:26, ". . . have ye not read in the book of Moses, how in the bush God spake unto him [Moses], saying, I am the God of Abraham, and the God of Isaac, and the God of Jacob?" (Mark 12:26).

Here Jesus vouches for the authenticity of Moses' record concerning the burning bush, quoting from Exodus 3:6. Or listen to Jesus after His resurrection as He converses with the travelers on the Emmaus Way: "And beginning at Moses and all the prophets, he expounded unto them in all the scriptures the things concerning himself" (Luke 24:27).

The disciples recognized the books of Moses and accepted them, for when they had met Jesus, Philip and Nathanael exclaimed: ". . . We have found him, of whom Moses in the law, and the prophets, did write . . ." (John 1:45).

In John 3:14 Jesus risks His reputation as Saviour upon the authority of Moses, and says: "And as Moses lifted up the serpent in the wilderness, even so must the Son of man be lifted up:

That whosoever believeth in him should not perish, but have eternal life" (John 3:14, 15).

As Moses—so Christ. If Moses' authority is questionable, so is Jesus'. But now listen to the all-conclusive, incontrovertible words of Christ as to the authority of the record of Moses:

> Search the scriptures; for in them ye think ye have eternal life: and they are they which *testify of me*.
> Do not think that I will accuse you to the Father: there is one that accuseth you, even *Moses*, in whom ye trust.
> For had ye believed Moses, ye would have believed me: for he wrote of me.
> But if ye believe not his writings, how shall ye believe my words? (John 5:39, 45-47).

## WHERE DID MOSES GET HIS INFORMATION?

We see then that Jesus endorsed the writings of Moses. He attached to them as much authority as to His own words. Since Jesus endorses the authority of Moses, He stakes His own claims of authority upon this fact. There is then no alternative to the question, "Is the record of Genesis, Exodus, Leviticus, Numbers, and Deuteronomy, true or false?" It is one or the other. Until you have settled this, there is no use going further. To show the need of a definite commitment on this issue, let us ask one question, "Where did Moses get his information?" He was born about two thousand years after the events of creation (re-creation) in Genesis 1:2-31. He was born three hundred years after the closing events recorded in Genesis 50. Where did Moses get all the information recorded in this first verse of the Bible and all that follows?

Skeptics and infidels have seized on this as conclusive proof that Moses could not have written Genesis. However, Jesus accepted the record. Many explanations have been put forward by ardent defenders of the Bible, claiming that there were written records *before* Moses' time and that Moses gleaned his information from these. Others assert that the information was handed down from generation to generation. Whether there be elements of truth or not in these explanations is of little consequence, for we do not need them. Moses received his information by direct *revelation*. Again and again we read, "And God spake unto Moses" (Exodus 6:2, 10, 13, 28, 29, etc., etc.). Whether God spake in an audible voice or by vision or by dream or by writing it out as in Deuteronomy 4:12, 13 makes no difference. It was God who spoke, and man's destiny depends on whether he believes God's Word or not. Do you believe the first words of Scripture, "In the beginning God created"? Then you too can believe on Him who said, "Except a man be born again, he cannot see the kingdom of God" (John 3:3). And He who said this was the same of whom Moses said, "In the beginning God." This God of the beginning in Genesis 1:1 is one with the One of whom John says,

> In the beginning was the Word, and the Word was with God, and the Word was God (John 1:1).
> . . . He that heareth my word, and believeth on him that sent me, hath everlasting life, and shall not come into condemnation; but is passed from death unto life (John 5:24).

*Chapter Six*

## THE QUESTION OF AUTHORITY

*In the beginning God created the heaven and the earth*
(Genesis 1:1).

Where did the universe come from? What is its origin? How
old is it? or is it without a beginning? These questions have occupied the minds of men since the dawn of human history. The
answers can be grouped under one of only two heads: *Creation*
or *Evolution*. It is one or the other. Either the record of Genesis
is true, or it is false. Creation and evolution cannot both be true.
The claim that theistic evolution is in harmony with the record
of the Bible is a totally indefensible claim. Quoting the International Standard Bible Encyclopedia, we declare:

> If the evolutionary conception is true, it naturally fol-
> lows that the Biblical account cannot be accepted liter-
> ally, for one of these accounts pictures the different
> species as developing gradually from pre-existent ones
> whereas the other [the Bible] clearly states they were
> individually created by a divine act (*International Stand-
> ard Bible Encyclopedia, vol. 2, p. 1046*).

The various species of plants and animals are the result of
definite acts of creation, and one species never evolves into
another. This is implied in the words, "after their kind." This
teaches the principle of heredity within the species.

All of it harks back to the authority of that first verse in the
Bible, "In the beginning God created." Right here in the very
opening statement, the Bible declares something which science
leaves totally untouched, and evolution persistently ignores and
evades. And that is the matter of "ultimate" origin. Where did
everything begin? The Bible asserts that the universe was
created out of nothing but God Himself. Evolution is defined
as a scientific and philosophical effort to explain the origin and

44

development of things in the universe. But this definition is not
entirely true, for evolution does not solve the question of ultimate origin. It does not begin with *nothing*, but assumes there
was *something* to begin with. It may go back and back and back
indefinitely, but it must assume there was something from which
everything came. It assumes the existence of substances and
forces working through successive transformations or evolutions,
but it poses or offers no answer to the problem of a first cause.
It begins with lifeless, inert matter or substance already existing,
but cannot go back beyond this. Here evolution stops, but the
Bible goes back to the ultimate beginning and gives the answer
in its opening statement, "In the beginning God created."

## THE GREAT QUESTION

An evolutionist said scoffingly to a Christian, "I simply cannot accept your doctrine of creation as stated in your Bible, for
it does not explain where God came from. If God created the
heaven and the earth, then tell me, Who created God?" Contemptuously he said, "Until you account for the existence of
God in the beginning I cannot accept it."

The Christian replied, "Before I answer you, I want to ask
you the same question. What is your explanation of the origin
of the universe and how do you account for us being here?"

To this the infidel confidently replied in the words of Huxley,
"The whole world living (organic) and non-living (inorganic)
is the result of the mutual attraction, according to definite laws
of the powers possessed by the molecules of which the primitive
nebulosity of the universe was composed."

"Yes, yes," replied the Christian. "But tell me, how did this
primitive nebulosity come to exist? Where did the molecules
originate and what produced the material attraction possessed
by the primitive nebulosity?"

To this the "would be" scientist replied, "Well, of course *that*
always was, and we don't know where it came from, so we assume it always existed."

"Indeed," replied the Christian. "You contemptuously ask me

to explain where God came from, and who made Him, and then you expect me to believe this nebulous, nebular, nebulosity theory."

Truly the words of Jesus do apply, "Ye . . . strain at a gnat, and swallow a camel" (Matthew 23:24). I do declare, it takes a thousand times more imagination and blind faith to believe this "non-luminous luminosity theory" than to believe the simple statement, "In the beginning God." Where the evolutionist stops —God begins! He cannot explain the origin of the universe, but the Bible answers it in the simple statement, "In the beginning God created."

## FOUNDATION OF FAITH

David says in Psalm 14:1, "The fool hath said in his heart, There is no God." Probably no victory of Satan in deceiving mankind since the fall in Eden has ever been so devastating as the modern substitution of the theories of evolution for the Word of God. For let us be perfectly clear in this, it is impossible to accept the modern theory of evolution concerning the origin of man, and also believe in the literal account of creation as given in the Bible. It is a repetition of the fall in the Garden of Eden. Of course, there is no room in evolution for an Eden, much less a fall of man, and still less for a plan of redemption. But notice the attack of Satan in the Garden. He said, "Ye shall be as gods" (Genesis 3:5). It was a suggestion of an evolution, man evolving and reaching the status of a god. That is evolution. If Satan can prove that man can "evolve" *into* a god, he will have little difficulty in proving that man evolved *from* a monkey. Satan's program is the exact opposite of God's program. The program of God begins with God, the Creator; Satan's begins with the creature and wants to work up to God, so that man is not only evolved from the lower animals, but ultimately God becomes the end product of this evolution of man.

## THE EVOLUTION OF EVOLUTION

The Apostle Paul describes for us the "evolution of the theory of evolution," for the theory of evolution is an evolution in itself.

Paul tells us how it came about in Romans 1:18-25. "For the wrath of God is revealed from heaven against all ungodliness and unrighteousness of men, who hold the truth in unrighteousness" (Romans 1:18).

Here Paul tells us that God is angry with men who "hold down" or "suppress" the truth. This is the literal rendering of the phrase, "who hold the truth in unrighteousness." It refers to a denial of the truth of God. In the next verse he gives the cause of God's wrath. It is: "Because that which may be known of God is manifest in them; for God hath shewed it unto them" (Romans 1:19).

The seriousness of man's rejection of the truth is evidenced by the fact that God has clearly manifested Himself. Man's reason alone is enough to condemn him for rejecting the truth of God. Man is an intelligent being, and to deny the truth of a God is unreasonable and a sure indication not of the evolution of man, but his degeneration. We might call it "devil-ution," for just as in the Garden of Eden, the word of the Devil was placed above the Word of God. And now Paul clinches the accusation of the folly of infidelity in verse 20: "For the invisible things of him from the *creation* of the world are clearly seen, being understood by the things that are made, even his eternal power and Godhead; so that they are without excuse" (Romans 1:20).

Creation is, in itself, a sufficient argument for the existence of a Creator. David says in Psalm 19, "The heavens declare the glory of God; and the firmament sheweth his handywork" (Psalm 19:1).

They are without excuse. To suppose that this great creation with its almost infinite diversity of planets, plants, animals, laws and manifestations, from the tiny atom to the gigantic sun, is the result of blind forces without an infinite, personal Intelligence guiding its courses, is folly and madness to the infinite degree. Science tells us that matter consists of elements composed of atoms, arranged in molecules which form the various known elements. Of these, less than one hundred are known to science (although others have been artificially produced). Yet out of these less than one hundred elements all matter is composed. By an almost infinite number of combinations we have all the different mineral, chemical, vegetable, and animal bodies, ranging from soil to trees, fish, birds, metals; in fact, every existing compound, millions of them, all subject to definite laws, following the laws of physics, genetics, and reproduction. Yet evolution would have us believe that all this organized creation evolved out of a disorganized nebular mass by residential forces.

To illustrate: There are twenty-six letters in the alphabet. Suppose we take fifty billion of each letter from A to Z and place them in a huge mixing bowl and start stirring them around. How long, do you imagine, would we have to stir these letters until we could expect the 23rd Psalm, or Milton's "Paradise Lost," or Shakespeare's "Macbeth" to come out, by the mere chance of the letters falling into their proper order to form the words? and then the words falling out in the proper order to form sentences? and the sentences by chance arranging themselves, to form the complete work? Yet this is a million times easier to believe than to believe that out of one hundred physical elements evolved a universe with plants, flowers, animals and birds, all subject to fixed laws and evident plan, and in almost infinite variety without a super-intelligent being at its source.

## BACK TO ROMANS

This is what Paul says in Romans 1. He says that those who deny the hand of the Creator in all this creation are without excuse and he calls them fools, instead of the intelligentsia which they imagine themselves to be. He therefore continues in Romans 1:21, "Because that, when they knew God, they glorified him not as God, neither were thankful; but became vain in their imaginations, and their foolish heart was darkened."

Instead of accepting the Word of God and glorifying Him, they became vain (proud) in their imaginations (their own speculations) and their eyes were closed to the revelation of God. And as a result, says Paul, they invented evolution. Did you ever carefully study Paul's description of evolution in

Romans 1, written almost two thousand years ago? Listen to it, and wonder:

> Professing themselves to be wise, they became fools [when they invented evolution],
> And changed the glory of the uncorruptible God into an image made like to corruptible man, and to birds, and fourfooted beasts, and creeping things (Romans 1:22,23).

Notice that we have here "evolution in reverse." It begins with God, descends to man, then to birds, then to beasts, and finally to creeping things. This is the real aim of evolution: to bring God down to their supposed beginning of things. We know evolution as the theory of beginning with a primitive cell and then evolving up to man, and finally man becoming God, but the real spirit of it as given by Paul is bringing God *down* and reducing Him to the level of creeping things. Turn Paul's order around and we have this order of evolution:

1. Creeping things
2. Fourfooted beasts
3. Flying birds
4. Man
5. God

You see then, evolution is the effort of man to create a God, and himself become God instead of accepting the Biblical account that God created man. For this reason, no Christian believer can accept the theory of modern evolution of man from a lower form of life, for it destroys the image of God. It leaves us without any explanation for the presence of evil and sin in the world; it cannot explain death, disease, suffering, and poverty. There is no room in the evolution of man from a beast for an atonement, a Cross, a Saviour, or a resurrection and future life. All these questions are left untouched by evolution, for in this theory of man evolving in the image of a monkey, there is no place for any of these things.

## BIBLE STANDS OR FALLS

One cannot believe modern evolution and also the Bible. They are irreconcilable. One or the other must go. No wonder then that, with the rise of evolution, the Bible has fallen into comparative disrepute. Today the Bible is banned in many of our public schools. When we remember that our school system was originally instituted by Christians who built their whole philosophy upon the dictum that the fear of the Lord is the beginning of wisdom, we wonder how it was possible that in a few brief years the Bible has been declared taboo in an increasing number of our schools. The answer is found in the acceptance of the evolutionary hypothesis. As the theory of evolution began to be taught in our schools and colleges, the Bible account had to go. Today evolution is freely taught from the kindergarten up, but the Bible — oh, no, no, no! That is unconstitutional. How is it that when the President of the United States takes the oath of office it must be done on the Bible, but our children must not be corrupted by it in our schools? How strange that infidels who cry bigotry, and will not tolerate the Bible account of Jesus Christ in our schools, will exploit the season of His birthday, Christmas, by keeping open their shops and stores seven days, eager to profit by the superstition(?) of Christians.

During World War II each soldier who went to war was given a copy of the New Testament, with the signature of President Franklin D. Roosevelt endorsing and recommending its use. Yes, the Bible was given by our President to the boys who went to face death on the battlefield, but *don't let our school children see this awful, dangerous Book!* Keep it away from our children. Give it instead to dying men. If the Bible had been made the foundation in our schools, our boys might not have had to die on the battlefield.

Thousands of Bibles are sent to our jails and penitentiaries for the men and women behind bars, and not one voice of protest is raised, but don't you dare give it to the boys and girls in our schools. How true the words of Paul, "Professing themselves to be wise, they became fools" (Romans 1:22). If we gave the Bible to the youngsters in school, there would be less call for them in our prisons and penitentiaries. And why has there been so little opposition to these increasing efforts to ban the Bible in our educational institutions? It is because we have submitted almost without a struggle or voice of protest to the tolerating of the ungodly teachings of an atheistic evolution. It is a sin which God must judge, and so Paul says again in Romans 1, "Wherefore God also gave them up . . ." (Romans 1:24).

And why? Listen! Because they: ". . . changed the truth of God into a lie [substituting evolution of man for creation by God], and worshipped and served the creature more than the Creator, who is blessed for ever. Amen" (Romans 1:25).

It may be too late, but I want my hands and conscience clean by lifting my voice against this corrupting cancer which has pervaded our society and is ripening it for certain judgment.

*Chapter Seven*

## TAKE IT OR LEAVE IT

*In the beginning God created the heaven and the earth* (Genesis 1:1).

Take it or leave it! There is the terse, final, uncompromising, dogmatic assertion with which the Bible opens. "In the beginning God created the heaven and the earth." Take it or leave it. Upon it God stakes His reputation. God will offer no explanation to meet man's curiosity; He will not waste time in giving details to satisfy man's credulity; He will not offer apologies for its lack of "how" God did it. He says so! We are expected to believe it because God says it. If you say you don't believe it, then I ask you for a better, a more logical explanation for the origin of the universe. And don't come with the speculations of atheistic evolution, for I have long since passed up that "monkey business" as totally discredited and unworthy of consideration.

And if you ask me why I accept the statement of Genesis 1:1 as fact, I reply that the One who said this is the only One who is qualified to make the statement, for He is the only One who was there when it happened. If you dispute the account of the One who made the worlds, I would ask, "Were you there? Have you talked to anyone else who was there?" Well, then I shall continue to believe the Word of the only One who was there.

### More Than Blind Faith

And so we believe that "In the beginning God created the heaven and the earth." A question naturally arises, a question we merely touched upon in our previous message. "Where did Moses get his information?" It must have been either by divine inspiration or revelation or else it cannot be accepted as genuine.

Moses recorded not only things which happened *before* he was born, he even recorded facts which antedated any traditions of his ancestors. But more than this, Moses also related some things before he died which did not happen until after he was dead.

For instance, Moses tells us of his own death and burial. This strange account of Moses has been seized upon by skeptics as definite proof that the book of Deuteronomy is a forgery, written after Moses was dead. The passage in question is in Deuteronomy 34. At the close of Moses' life God led him up to Mount Nebo and there showed him the promised land. And then while there on the mountain alone with God, Moses died and was buried by God, and no one knew where his grave was located. How do we know all this if there was no one there to witness this closing scene in the life of Moses? Higher critics loudly assert, "This proves the record as false. How could anyone report the death and burial of Moses if he was not there himself?" But instead of disproving the record, this account *proves* divine inspiration, for this account was written by Moses himself *before he went up into the mountain to die.*

How did Moses know? By divine revelation just as he received all the rest of the information contained in the five books of Moses, which were endorsed by the Lord Jesus. Instead of evidence of forgery, the very account of Moses by himself concerning his death and burial is an unassailable proof of inspiration. But even if the account were written by another, it would still have to be by inspiration. In the same way Moses received by divine revelation the information, "In the beginning God created the heaven and the earth." Moses therefore records things which happened before he was born and after he was dead. Upon this revelation rests the whole volume of prophecy written by men who lived and died before it came to pass.

## ARCHEOLOGY

To the believer these things present no problem, for once we have believed the opening statement of the Bible, "In the beginning God created the heaven and the earth," we can believe anything this great sovereign Creator says. But that the infidel may have no excuse, creation itself testifies to both the existence and greatness of God. David says, "The heavens declare the glory of God; and the firmament sheweth his handywork" (Psalm 19:1).

Paul tells us:

> Because that which may be known of God is manifest in them; for God hath shewed it unto them.
> For the invisible things of him from the creation of the world are clearly seen, being understood by the things that are made, even his eternal power and Godhead; so that they are without excuse (Romans 1:19, 20).

Atheistic evolution is without excuse because it even denies *two things* for which no revelation is needed. Creation alone, wholly apart from any other revelation, is sufficient to show an intelligent being two things about the originator of the universe. These two things are *power* and *personality*. Whoever created this world must be a *person* and be a person of *power*. I know that behind my watch is a watch-maker. It didn't just happen. It was made by a person, and that person must have had intelligence. Common sense also tells me that that tree which I see out of my window did not just happen; there is someone who made that tree. And it tells me not only of a God of power but a God of wisdom, for next to that pine tree grows an entirely different tree, a maple, and twenty feet from that maple is a stately elm tree. All are planted in the same soil, receive the same rain and sunlight, yet have different shapes, different leaves, and exude different sap: gum from the pine and full of turpentine; sap from the maple, full of sugar. Yet both have their roots in the same soil, drink the same rain, absorb the same sunlight. Did this just happen? No, says Paul; they all speak of a Creator who says, "In the beginning God." Man is without excuse!

## EDUCATED FOOLISHNESS

It is a strange paradox that the more human wisdom a man achieves, the more stupid he often becomes. One would think that a doctor, an anatomist, a scientist, a chemist, would be the first to admit that there is a God of wisdom, power, order and design, and yet such is the perversity of human nature that some of the wisest men of the world have been the greatest infidels and skeptics. A person may be the most brilliant genius in the arts and the sciences and yet fail to see the supernatural in the Bible. Of course, we know the answer, for "the wisdom of this world is foolishness with God" (I Corinthians 3:19). Jesus said, "Except a man be born again, he cannot see" (John 3:3). The natural man is blind to spiritual things; and so the unregenerate man, no matter how astute, educated, and intelligent, will remain in total darkness concerning the spiritual content of the Bible until his eyes are opened *by faith in the Word of God*. When a man will admit that God knows more about this Book He Himself has written than he does, God will open his eyes to understand what he believes, for says the writer of Hebrews, "*Through faith* we understand that the worlds were framed by the word of God" (Hebrews 11:3).

But even though a person may be blind to spiritual truth because he is unregenerate, his eyes are open to natural evidences round about him. Nature witnesses to its Creator. Creation declares a revelation of God. Wherever man is found there is this recognition of a God in nature. Higher education without spiritual sight therefore makes fools of men who deny the revelations of God. There are no atheists among the primitive nations of the earth. They have enough sense, not yet spoiled by "science, so called," to doubt the existence of God. Wherever man is found you will find him acknowledging and worshiping a god of some kind. It may be only a mountain, an animal, or a man-made idol, but he owns a god. From the ice-bound regions of the Arctic to the sweltering, steaming jungle glades of the Equator, where there is a man, there is a belief in God.

## BIBLE REVELATION

But in addition to this innate consciousness concerning the existence of God, we have an infallible revelation of God. While it is true that the Bible is primarily a *revelation*, and not a scientific treatise of the origin of things, it is nevertheless as infallible when it speaks on the subject of geology, mathematics, chemistry, physics, geography, psychology, or physiology, as when it deals with salvation. To the open mind this supernatural character of the Bible must be apparent. Written over a period of almost two thousand years by some forty different writers, from peasants to kings, and in several different lands, and under the widest, most divergent political and social conditions, yet there is no conflict, no contradiction, but all are in harmony and agreement.

John in Revelation does not negate a single statement by Moses in Genesis. The teachings of Jesus did not in one single instance disprove anything Moses wrote two thousand years before. Compare this with the discoveries and speculations of men. Apply this to the various theories of evolution which were at one time or another accepted as valid, and yet have been disproven in a succeeding generation. No two exponents of evolution have ever fully agreed. Beginning with Aristotle four hundred years before Christ until today, no single theory of the evolutionist's explanation for the existence of man has been accepted for more than a few years; sooner or later each theory is rejected and proved false. Aristotle thought he had proved the evolution of life by spontaneous generation when he supposed that the appearance of maggots in spoiling meat generated spontaneously from no previously existing life. But then came the discovery by Francesco Redi that the maggots which became flies were hatched from the eggs of flies who came from other maggots, laid by previous generations of flies, etc., etc., etc., and Aristotle's proof of abiogenesis or spontaneous generation went the way of all flesh. Spencer did not agree with Darwin; Huxley disputed much that Spencer taught, and so on, with all the other names in the field of evolution. But not so with the Bible. Moses who wrote four thousand years ago has never yet been proved to have been mistaken in a single instance, whether he wrote on medicine, surgery, physics, geography, or redemption. It has never needed revision. It stands!

Before concluding this chapter we want to point out the seriousness of giving ear to the teachings of evolution. We repeat, that if the evolutionary theory of the origin of man by evolution from lower animals were ever proved as true, it would automatically disprove the Bible, and reduce it to an antiquated compilation of superstitions, fables, and fancies unworthy of a place in human history. We mention here just one aspect of the incompatibility of evolution and the Scriptures, on which we hope to elaborate in our coming messages. If we must accept the theory that man evolved from an animal ancestor by a developmental process, then the literal account of Genesis 1 cannot be true. "And God said, Let us make man in our image, after our likeness: . . . So God created man in his own image, in the image of God created he him" (Genesis 1:26, 27).

Atheistic evolution would substitute the image of a monkey for the "image of God." Then, too, there is no room for a "fall," for evolution teaches a development *upward* and not a fall downward to total depravity. Evolution has no place for sin and subsequently no place for an atonement, and since there is no need for an atonement, there is no need for a Saviour. To the problem of sin and where it came from, evolution says, "All the evil and violence and bad tendencies in man are the remnants and carry-over or survival of his ancestral traits. Cruelty, lust, and deceitfulness are but the residue of the 'tiger and the ape' in man, and as he evolves still more he will finally also get rid of these, just as we have lost our tails in the process of evolving upward." But if this be true, that we are evolving upward, how do you account for the fact that man at the top of the evolutionary ladder is guilty of crimes and cruelties no respectable animal would stoop to do or consider? It is rather humorously expressed, yet with a pungently serious application, in a poem I read years ago:

> Three monkeys sat in a coconut tree,
>   Looking down on people like you and me.
> Said one to the other, Now listen you,
>   There's a certain rumor that can't be true,
> That man descended from our noble race;
>   The very idea is a rank disgrace.
>
> No monkey ever deserted his wife,
>   Starved her babies and ruined her life.
> And you've never seen a mother monk
>   To leave her babies with others to bunk;
> With baby sitters of one sort or another,
>   Till they scarcely know who is their mother.

And another thing you'll never see,
   A monk build a fence round a coconut tree;
And let the coconuts go to waste,
   Rather than let someone else have a taste;
Why, if I'd put a fence around my tree,
   I'd only invite you to steal from me.

Here's another thing a monk won't do,
   Go out at night and come home in a stew.
Or use a gun, a club or a knife,
   To take some other monkey's life.
Yes, man descended, the ornery cuss,
   But he surely never descended from us.

I'd rather believe the monkey than those who disgrace the monkeys by trying to horn in on their family tree.

## Chapter Eight

## EVIDENCES OF INSPIRATION

*In the beginning God created the heaven and the earth*
(Genesis 1:1).

This is God's first and final word concerning the origin of the universe. No attempt is made to explain it, no apologies for lack of detail; just the final, conclusive word of the Creator, "In the beginning God." It still stands as the simplest, yet the most logical explanation for the existence of all things. Compare this simple statement with the explanation for this world by the renowned scientist Herbert Spencer. He says in explaining how the earth originated: "The integration of matter out of an indefinite, incoherent homogeneity into definite, coherent heterogeneity with concomitant dissipation of energy."

Today science acknowledges that there is nothing to support the theory of "spontaneous generation"; that is, that living matter can come out of non-living substances. Biogenesis, the doctrine that living organisms can proceed only from or be generated by living parents, germs, or organisms, still stands as the only explanation for life. Since there can be no life without antecedent life, we must push back the process to the ultimate source of life. We must begin with life. Science pushes it back to a primordial germ, to a mass of protoplasm, but without explaining where or when this primordial germ received its life. Only the Bible gives the answer, "In the beginning God created the heaven and the earth." And this God was life, and man received his life from the Author of life and the source and beginning of all life. Of this Creator John tells us: "All things were made by him; and without him was not any thing made that was made. In him was life; and the life was the light of men" (John 1:3, 4).

59

## MOSES THE SCIENTIST

It was Moses who first laid down this principle of life. Before life could be created, there must be a living Creator and this Moses asserts was *in the beginning*. On this statement the veracity of the entire Bible rests. With the truth of Genesis 1:1 the whole structure of our faith stands or falls. We dare to risk the authenticity of the Bible, our eternal destiny, our salvation, our whole system of Christian doctrine on the words of Moses as recorded in the five books of the Pentateuch which opens with the unequivocal, incontrovertible statement, "In the beginning God created the heaven and the earth."

We would remind you that Moses wrote the books of Genesis, Exodus, Leviticus, Numbers, and Deuteronomy, four thousand years ago. Not four hundred, not forty years ago, but four thousand. Books written on science four hundred years ago or even forty years ago, are completely out of date today, and must either be scrapped or revised to conform with subsequent discoveries. But here are five books which were written four thousand years ago, on practically every subject, and yet have never needed revision. When Moses wrote, modern science was still unknown. Practically all the beliefs of those dim days have been abandoned. Yet Moses was educated and trained in all the wisdom of the Egyptians. Stephen tells us in Acts 7 that, "Moses was learned in all the wisdom of the Egyptians, and was mighty in words and in deeds" (Acts 7:22).

The word "learned" in this verse means educated or instructed, and is so translated in some versions. Notice one other word, *all*. Moses was educated in *all* the branches of learning in Egypt. And what did the "educators" of that day teach? What did the Egyptian scientists teach concerning the practice of medicine, in which I naturally am quite interested? Most diseases were supposed to be demon-caused, and so incantations, fetishes, charms and witchcraft were employed freely. Bloodletting, that is, bleeding of patients was freely practiced, whereas today we have reversed the whole thing and give transfusions, the very opposite of bloodletting. It was taught that the seat of life was in the liver or even the bowels. Today we have found out it is in the blood. Diseases were treated long after the days of Moses by such crude remedies as powdered toad skins, by the murder of supposed witches, and by mutilating, blistering, and cauterizing to drive out demons. We ask the question, since Moses was educated in all these superstitions and primitive practices, how does it happen that he does not teach or recommend these remedies in his writings? Although he deals in detail and great length with diseases, the treatment of infections, leprosy, and running sores, yet the illusions, deceptions, gross errors, and superstitions concerning anatomy, physiology, pathology, and treatment of diseases as taught in the highest schools of learning in Egypt from which Moses was a graduate, are never taught or even suggested in the books of Moses. But instead the instructions Moses laid down for Israel were utterly at variance with the accepted practices of that day, and fully in harmony with modern-day scientific facts. Where did Moses get his knowledge of bacteriology thirty-five hundred years before its discovery by Louis Pasteur as late as the nineteenth century? Where did Moses get his knowledge of blood and circulation millenniums before William Harvey discovered the circulation of the blood in the seventeenth century? Where did Moses get his knowledge of sterilization and disinfection and quarantine for communicable diseases, when science had only known what Moses taught for a little over one hundred years when Joseph Lister introduced antiseptic surgery?

## Moses Knew It All

Where did Moses get his knowledge? From the universities of Egypt? Hardly, for it was thousands of years before scientists caught up with Moses. Let me give some illustrations. Take the science of prophylaxis — the prevention of disease. Not only was the special diet Moses described a proven aid to good health, but Moses also knew about bacteriology and the spread of disease by contact and infection and so instructed quarantine measures and isolation. Israelites with leprosy were carefully isolated (quarantined). Others with communicable diseases were carefully guarded from spreading the disease, and their clothing, dishes and utensils were sterilized by heat. After an infectious disease, the patient must be kept isolated for an additional week, and then thoroughly washed in running water. Did it ever occur to you why the Israelite, having had an infection, was to wash in *running water* (Leviticus 15:13)? It was to wash away dangerous bacteria. If you have ever watched a modern surgeon prepare for an operation, you will see him place his hands under the tap, which has been turned on with his knee or foot, and scrub and scrub his hands for five to fifteen minutes under *running* water. But why running water? Why not in a bowl? Because dangerous bacteria are present on the hands and washing in a bowl of water would only pollute the water the moment the hands touched it, and no amount of washing in that polluted water can result in the hands becoming surgically clean. So it is done under running water and the germs are carried away. Well, Moses knew all this (Leviticus 15:13).

## TRUE IN EVERY FIELD

Modern medicine has not been able to point to one single instruction given by Moses relative to the treatment of disease, method of surgery, quarantine, sterilization or hygiene, which is not true and applicable today. And this holds true for every field of scientific discovery. Anatomists today have found that man's body is composed of the same elements as the ground on which we walk, but Moses said that four thousand years ago: "And God formed man out of the dust of the ground."

We ask again, How is it that Moses and the other Bible writers escaped the errors and superstitions of their contemporaries? What was it that guarded these Bible writers against the foolish traditions of their time, or kept them from conflicting with one another when separated by hundreds of years? There is but one answer — supernatural inspiration — *REVELATION!*

To produce further evidence hardly seems necessary, for the subject is inexhaustible. However, we mention just one more evidence. In the realm of law and jurisprudence we have a revelation given four thousand years ago which has never required alteration. The laws of Moses form the vital principles of all legal science — judicial, national, and international. Where did Moses get these laws which antedated and surpassed all the wisdom and philosophy of the most enlightened ages, and forms the basis of jurisprudence of all the courts in the world?

Because of all this evidence of the authenticity of the revelation of the books of Moses, I dare to believe, in the face of ridicule, inviting abject pity, suffering the sneers of infidels, braving the accusation of being an antiquated, ancient, mossbacked fossil — I say, I still dare to believe the Bible when it says, "In the beginning God created the heaven and the earth," and that God "created man in his own image." Infidels may scoff and sneer and try to make a monkey out of me, but I shall stake my destiny on "Thus saith the Lord."

## NATURAL HISTORY

Do you know that the Old Testament alone contains more than two hundred and fifty botanical terms and names of plants and trees and flowers from the great cedar of Lebanon to the humble hyssop in the wall? Yet under the careful scrutiny of the most exacting botanists, the description of the flora of the Bible never makes one slip or mistake. The same is true of the fauna of the Bible. The zoological science of the Bible is as foolproof as the botanical. Under the most critical scrutiny and recent examination of the Bible, though describing all sorts of animal life from the leviathan to the snail, from the lion to the moth in the garment, the Bible descriptions are found to be above criticism. Until recently avian scientists taught that, in the words of the poet, the vulture could "scent the carrion from afar," being able to smell the carcasses of beasts, but now science has exploded this theory and reveals that the vulture's keenness of sight rather than its acuteness of smell enables it to detect its food afar off. But Job already stated this three thousand years ago (Job 28:7).

In the field of meteorology the Bible is equally infallible. Solomon describes evaporation and rainfall (Ecclesiastes 1:7). He already described the recurring prevailing wind (Ecclesiastes 1:6). He knew about the laws of condensation (Job 26:8). When we turn to the field of geology we again find *revelation* thousands of years ahead of modern education. Plato tells us that the Egyptians taught that the earth originated in a kind of pulp; and that men were generated from the slime of the river

Nile. Others taught that the world was hatched from a winged egg. Now remember that this was the current belief in Egypt, as taught in their schools when Moses was going to school. Moses was educated in these schools, and we ask again, How does it come about that Moses, while he himself was rescued from the slime of the river Nile, did not make the mistake of saying that man originated from that same slime? How does it happen that he did not record the world as being hatched from a winged egg, but instead says, "In the beginning God created," and "in his image he created man"? Remember, Moses was learned (educated) in all the wisdom of the Egyptians.

In regard to the earth, all sorts of foolish notions were held when the Bible was written. Some held the earth was flat; others thought it like a drum. Ancient sages taught the earth rested on the back of a huge turtle and the turtle rested on the coils of a huge serpent. It must have been thus, for if not, then what does it rest upon? Others believed the earth was supported on the backs of huge elephants, the motion of their heads producing earthquakes. As late as 400 A.D. St. Augustine taught that there was no life on the underside of the earth because of its darkness. To refuse this explanation was gross heresy and grounds for excommunication as an infidel.

Even Christian theologians as late as Galileo's time taught that the earth was stationary, that the moon was a mixture of air and fire, that comets were the souls of men on their way to Heaven. Others said they were angels escorting righteous souls to places of rest. And so we might go on and on, but we return to the question, how is it that the Bible, written by men who lived in an age when these things were believed and taught as fact, never once made the mistake of stating that the earth was flat, but instead tells us it was round like a circle (Isaiah 40:22)? And Job tells us that instead of the earth resting on the back of tortoises or elephants, the "earth hangeth upon nothing," that is, suspended in space (Job 26:7).

## No Excuse

Before closing this chapter (and we might pile up the evidences of the supernatural inspiration of the Book) we must make the application to the individual. The Bible is not only the final and authoritative word on the matters we have discussed, but it is pre-eminently God's Book of salvation, and all these other revelations are secondary in importance and are incidental to the message of redemption which is the purpose of the Book. The evidence of its supernatural character applies also to the finality of God's way of salvation. This Bible teaches that God created man in His image, that man fell in sin and came under judgment of death, and was destined for an eternal Hell in outer darkness. The Bible then teaches that God provided a way of salvation by sending His Son into the world to die for these sinners, to put away the sin problem so that all who believe the Word of God, the promises of God, may obtain eternal life, escape a future destiny in Hell, and become the children of God. If you will believe this and accept it, you can be saved. But you cannot believe just what you choose. You must believe all God says, for if the Bible is not *all* God's Word, then who can tell which is, and which is *not*? You must begin with Genesis 1:1, "In the beginning God created the heaven and the earth." If *you* believe this, then you can also believe that Jesus Christ is *this* Creator, for John says: "In the beginning was the Word, and the Word was with God, and the Word was God. All things were made [created] by him [the Word]; and without him was not any thing made that was made" (John 1:1, 3).

This Word is Jesus Christ, for John 1:14 says, "And the Word was made flesh, and dwelt among us."

Jesus Christ was the Word of God incarnate who was the Creator in Genesis 1:1. The Creator God of Genesis 1:1 is one with the Creator Word of John 1:1. If you do not believe Genesis 1:1, you cannot believe that John 1:3 refers to Jesus Christ without whom there is no salvation. Why not receive Him now, and say, "I do believe, I do receive Jesus Christ as my Saviour, and by faith in the Word of God trust Him to keep me for eternity"?

*Chapter Nine*

# EVOLUTION OR CREATION?

Where did this universe originate? Where did it come from and out of what was it made? Is there an answer to these questions, and how can we know which is the right one? There are, generally speaking, only two answers — creation and evolution. The Bible asserts that this universe is the product of a supernatural act of creation. The Bible makes the plain, direct, unapologetic, dogmatic assertion, "In the beginning God created the heaven and the earth" (Genesis 1:1). It then goes on to say that the plants, the fishes, the birds and mammals were created on separate days as distinct creations, and finally man was created by God breathing His Spirit into a mass of clay and thus man came into being in the image of God. Once this account of creation is literally accepted, our search for the answers to our questions concerning the origin of the universe is at an end.

## SECOND ANSWER

There is, however, another answer which man brings forward to account for this world, its occupants, and man. This we call the hypothesis or theory of evolution, a term which is difficult to define because scientists differ so widely among themselves regarding the steps and pattern of the evolution of things in the universe. In general, however, we may accept Darwin's definition (*Origin of the Species,* p. 523). He defines evolution as:

"the belief that all animals and plants are descended from some single primordial form."

It endorses the doctrine that all species, including man, are descended from other lower species, all changes in the organic world being the result of natural law and *not of miraculous interposition*. The line of descent varies with different scientists but generally begins with primitive protozoa, evolving into

66

worms; worms into fish; fish into amphibians; amphibians into reptiles; reptiles into birds and mammals; and finally mammals into man; and man into — what? Why doesn't the process continue? Science doesn't answer.

From this it will be seen that the record of creation in Genesis and the theories of evolution are in direct conflict, and we must accept one or the other. Both cannot be true. One is false, and we want to know which one. Evolutionists and creationists both realize that the theory of evolution and the literal account of creation in Genesis are mutually exclusive. If evolution is true, not only is the Bible in error in its account of creation, but all the rest which follows in the Bible regarding the fall, redemption and salvation are also untrue and unnecessary. It was none other than H. G. Wells, author of *The Outline of History* who once wrote:

> If all animals and man evolved . . then there were no first parents, no paradise, no fall. And if there had been no fall, then the entire historic fabric of Christianity, the story of the first sin, and the reason for an atonement collapses like a house of cards.

To which we say "amen," for the descendants of monkeys have no need for a Saviour. How would it sound to quote I Timothy 1:15, "this is a faithful saying, and worthy of all acceptation, that Christ Jesus came into the world to save monkeys"?

## GENESIS AN ALLEGORY?

There are, however, some who call themselves evolutionists who violently object to the charge that the Bible account of creation and evolution are in conflict. When we boldly assert that one cannot believe the Bible and be an evolutionist, or be an evolutionist and believe the Bible, they rise up in righteous indignation and accuse us either of ignorance or bigotry. "Why," says one man, "I am an evolutionist and I too believe the Bible." Indeed? Do you mean to tell me that you believe the literal account of creation in six days, and also believe that man evolved from some lower order of organic life in a period spanning millions of years? That seems like a contradiction. "Oh, no," says my Bible-believing(?) evolutionist friend. "You see, I believe the account of Genesis, but I don't believe it is to be taken literally. It is an allegory; it is figurative, and we must interpret it figuratively." Says my friend, "I am not an atheist. I am a theistic evolutionist. I believe that in the beginning God created something, and then left this something to develop and evolve into something else, a living cell which evolved into a primitive animal, and so on up until we reach man. You see, I am not an atheist. I believe in God; that is, a god of evolution."

Now all this sounds fine, but it just will not stand the test of careful examination. Let me ask you, my friend, where in your theistic evolution do you find a place for a *fall* of man as described in Genesis 3? When man fell, he fell *down — not up* to a higher form! The fall was not evolution; but degeneration. Where is there room in theistic evolution for man created in the image of God? Where is there a need for God incarnate in His creature? How can you account for sin, for death, for the problem of good vs. evil? Where is there a place for redemption, for Calvary, for a resurrection? Away with your silly drivel about theistic evolution. All evolution is atheistic in the final analysis, for it basically denies the Word of God.

## THE EVOLUTIONIST'S ANSWER

But my evolutionist friend, unwilling to yield, still holds to his point and says, "We must not take the Bible account of creation as literal, but symbolic and allegorical." But where does the symbolic and allegorical stop? If the first chapter of Genesis is an allegory, and does not describe what actually happened, how then can I take anything else which follows literally? Then the story of the fall too is an allegory. Then the story of Cain and Abel is fiction. Then the record of Israel's deliverance from Egypt and their establishment in Palestine was not literally true. Then the story of the birth of Jesus is an allegory. Do you see, my friend, that to reject one part of the Bible makes every other part unreliable, for who after all is the authority to tell us which is literal and which must be spiritualized?

We therefore repeat, one cannot believe in evolution, be it atheistic or theistic, and also believe the Bible literally. There can be no Christian evolutionists. Evolution, stripped of all its pseudo-scientific claims, all its theoretical evidence, all of its insults to the Bible, is in the end a Satanic attempt to get rid of God, and finally produce a super-race of supermen, who will be gods themselves. If the theory of the "survival of the fittest" resulting in an ever-mounting process of higher and higher creatures is true, then there is some argument in favor of allowing only the fittest to reproduce and thus speed up the process toward a super-race of men. And, in fact, this has already been put forward. In the book, *Evolution and Human Destiny*, the author suggests this horrible, gruesome proposition:

> The further evolution of human society would be greatly affected by the development of a reproductive system operating on a social level. An entirely different situation would prevail were it possible to sire future humanity from the best fraction of one percent of humanity (*Evolution and Human Destiny* by Kohler, pp. 107-109).

Think of that! Pick out a fraction of one percent of the most highly developed and cultured people in a community and allow only these to reproduce and act as parents of all future children, while all who did not pass the examination for intellectual, physical, or cultural fitness would be prohibited from reproducing. Sterilization of 499 out of every 500 might then be the answer. Gruesome as this suggestion is, it is only a logical conclusion if the theories of evolution contain any truth at all, and survival of the fittest is the only answer.

## WHAT IS THE ANSWER?

Before we close this chapter we must, however, give a word of warning and of explanation. There is much which goes under the name of evolution which is not evolution, but should be called development or improvement instead. The Bible statement, "Let it bring forth after its kind," does not preclude the development of a wide range of varieties within that particular species or kind. Unfortunately a great deal of misunderstanding has resulted from use of the term "evolution" to denote mere improvement of a species or the development of new varieties of the same species. There are many varieties of the same species; for instance, there are different kinds of apples, or different kinds of pickles. We have within the canine or dog species many varieties: foxes, wolves, and dingoes, from the diminutive Mexican Chihuahua to the massive St. Bernard, or Great Dane, but they are all dogs. So there are many varieties of cats within the feline kind, such as the different breeds of domestic cats: Siamese, Angora, and Maltese, not to mention other members of the family such as lions, leopards, tigers, wild cats, etc. But all are still cats. All the varieties of apples came from one original kind of apple, but by culture and scientific pollination and grafting were developed into greatly improved different varieties. But this is not evolution; this is merely improvement, development, and cultivation.

Evolution teaches the change or transmutation by means of a slow process of one species into another, from a lower to a higher, resulting in an entirely new kind, such as a fish into a mammal, or a goat into a cow, or a hippopotamus into a horse, or a monkey into a man. This is quite a different thing than cultivating new varieties of the same species. Not one single proven example of an evolution from one species to another has ever been found. The missing link is a link which is entirely in the realm of supposition without one single speck of tangible proof. We therefore do not reject an "evolution" which refers to a development or improvement within the species, but we do reject an evolution which assumes a transgression of the basic, inviolable law of God, "Let it bring forth after its kind."

Today science must abide by that law, "like produces like"; or "everything after its kind." Not one example of evolution of a lower order of beings into a higher has yet been found. The whole theory is built upon speculative and dubious findings of parts of organisms in a state of decay and only remotely related to each other. Science today itself defines a species as a group capable of reproducing offspring of any two parents. This fertility determines and proves that the parents were of the same species. Members of two different species usually cannot interbreed, but even in the rare cases where two very closely related species can reproduce, the resulting offspring is sterile and the evolutionist theory is stopped at its outset. As an example we have the mule, which is the offspring of a jackass and a mare, but is completely sterile and cannot reproduce, thus making impossible the emergence of a new species. Since members of different species (*kinds* in Bible language) do not interbreed, there can be no evolution. Without a change or production of a new species, there can be no evolution; therefore, the theory of evolution is not only unscriptural but it is utterly unscientific, unproven and contrary to all scientific facts and logic.

## AN APPLICATION

Finally, we object to and reject the theory of evolution because it destroys the plan of salvation by a creative act of God in regeneration. The Devil has been quick to apply evolution also to God's revelation concerning the new creation. Jesus said, "Except a man be born again, he cannot see the kingdom of God" (John 3:3). It does not say, Except a man gradually improve, he cannot see the kingdom of God. Paul says, "If any man be in Christ he is a new creation." Satan would have us substitute a spiritual evolution in place of a creative act. According to spiritual evolution there is no need for regeneration but only an evolution or cultivation of the natural, latent virtues in the heart of man. Modern theology would substitute a cultural, moral, social evolution for the new birth, and begins with the creature instead of the Creator. Natural, material evolution begins with a primordial cell instead of with God. So too in the spiritual, infidels begin with man, teaching that by his works, religion, and human merit, he finally earns for himself a salvation obtained by human efforts and self-improvement. We hear a great deal about the dignity and divinity of man and the universal Fatherhood of God, but God says there is no evolution from the natural to the spiritual, from sinner to saint. Jesus settled it once for all when He said: "That which is born of the flesh is flesh; and that which is born of the Spirit is spirit" (John 3:6).

Flesh is flesh, and never will be anything else. Spirit is spirit, and always was. Flesh does not evolve into spirit. They are forever different, and God's original law of creation still stands, "Let it bring forth after its kind."

Like produces like; that which is born of the flesh is (remains) flesh; and that which is born of the Spirit is spirit.

YE MUST BE BORN AGAIN!

## Chapter Ten

## MUTATIONS, YES! TRANSMUTATIONS, NO!

*In the beginning God created the heaven and the earth*
(Genesis 1:1).

The human mind is incapable of conceiving of or even im-
agining the existence of anything without a beginning, and so
concerning every existing thing the question naturally arises,
Where did it come from? where did it begin? However, the
ultimate answer to this question can never be reached by the
human mind by reason alone, for it reaches into infinity; and
the human mind being finite and limited is unable to compre-
hend a beginningless past, just as he cannot grasp the idea of
limitless space. If he could reach the beginning, he would still
be faced with the question, Where did the beginning come
from? Let us accept the theory of a primordial germ as the beginning of all life and suppose that everything started from one
single germ cell; then we have not yet answered the question,
Where did this primordial cell come from? Or if we assume the
nebular hypothesis as the beginning of the universe, we must
still answer the question, Where did the original fire-mist come
from?

### THE BIBLE BEGINNING

Of course, we must admit that we are confronted with the
same identical problem if we accept the Bible answer, "In the
beginning God." We are still faced with the questions, "How
did God begin? Where did God come from? Who made God?"
These cannot be answered logically but must be accepted by
faith. The Bible assumes that God always was. It teaches that
He had no beginning, but always existed from eternity. This,
of course, we cannot understand, and never will, but it is the

plain teaching of the Book. Moses says in the second verse of Psalm 90: "Before the mountains were brought forth, or ever thou hadst formed the earth and the world, even from everlasting to everlasting, thou art God."

But even if it were possible to answer the question, Who made God? it would still solve nothing, for we would still have to answer the question, Who made the one who made God? and so we could go on into infinity. The Bible, therefore, leaves the subject with this simple, dogmatic statement, "In the beginning God." We grant that it does not answer a thousand other questions which carry us back to an incomprehensible infinity, but it is still the best answer to the origin of this universe.

We admit that accepting the record of the Bible leaves us with the same question as the theory of evolution, but comparison of the two makes the Bible answer the only one that can satisfy. Which is the most logical—to begin with a blob of mud, or begin with an omnipotent, omniscient, eternal God? When I come to God I reach the end of my search, and I rest; when I come to the original blob of protoplasm I am still bogged down in the fog of doubts and questions.

## COMPARE EVOLUTION

The choice is between the Word of God and the speculations of man. It is a question of believing the Creator or the creature. Evolution in its search for the ultimate origin must eventually come to God, or forever flounder about in the mists of hypotheses, speculations, and transient guesses. Either God is right or wrong. Both creation and evolution cannot be right. However, when we use the term evolution, we must again remind you what we mean by the term, for in a sense there is evolution — definite development and an evolving of organisms from one level of development to another. There is an evolution which is in perfect harmony with the Bible. We reject, however, that particular theory of evolution which does not begin with a personal, eternal, all-wise, all-powerful God as the Creator of the universe. This we call atheistic evolution, which traces the origin of everything to an inert, brainless mass of fire-mist, or protoplasm, or a primordial germ cell, without the creative act of a sovereign God. This we reject as an utterly untenable position.

## Theistic Evolution

We have already mentioned a second theory of evolution which assumes that there is a God, a personal Creator in the beginning. We call it "theistic evolution." It accepts the premise that in the beginning God created the universe or earth and then left it to develop according to certain inherent created laws placed within matter by God. This theory assumes that the universe is like a clock which the manufacturer winds up and then lets it run by itself. This is the teaching of deism. There is another form of theistic evolution which goes a little farther but not far enough. It teaches that God did create the original earth, but then supposes that all subsequent plant and animal life evolved under the hand of God from a lower form to a higher without separate creative acts for each species. One can be a theistic evolutionist, believe in God as Creator and yet hold that everything evolved from the original mass beginning with protozoa, developing into worms, worms into fish, fish into amphibians and then into reptiles, birds and mammals and finally *MAN*. But the Bible says that the creation of plants, fish and birds, animals and man, were separate acts of God, each after its kind and not an evolving of one into another and merging of a lower into a higher. We therefore cannot accept theistic evolution because it is in direct conflict, not necessarily with the creation of the world in Genesis 1:1 but in the way in which God populated this earth. What shall we believe, "So God created man in his own image," or the definition of Darwin, "all animals and plants are descended from some one primordial form, and evolving in a chain of links one resulting from another"?

## A Word of Caution

God's Word definitely states that birds and fish did not evolve from trees and plants, and mammals and beasts did not evolve from fish and birds, and certainly not that man gradually evolved from the ape. They are separate acts of God, on separate days. Each order was set apart without a link between them, to be kept forever from developing from one kind to the other. This is clinched by the *TEN TIMES* repeated expression in the first chapter of Genesis, "after its kind." Everything was to be *after its kind*. The word kind means "species." Each species of plant, fish, fowl, and animal was to reproduce only *its own kind* and never produce any other "kind." This alone is incontrovertible proof, there can be no crossing over of the species, no evolving of one kind into another, or transmutation.

As we have emphasized before, it is unfortunate that so much confusion has come from the use of the word "evolution" to denote mere improvement *within* the species or the development of new varieties within the *kind* or species. We know there are, through years of development, numerous varieties within each species, different kinds of cats and dogs, ducks and chickens, but they never evolve from one to the other. The different varieties of cats are still all cats, whether they are house cats, bob cats, wild cats, Siamese cats or Angora cats. There is diversity of kind and improvement within each species (called "kind" in Genesis 1), but this is not what we mean by evolution. Our controversy is not over the improvement of a species, by interbreeding, cultivation, by mutations and selective breeding, or other means, to produce new and better "varieties" of any species, but over the evolution of one *species* into another — a cat into a horse, or a monkey into a man. The God-given rule, "Let it bring forth after its kind," is inviolable and stands as an adamant insurmountable barrier against all our modern theories of evolution. The missing link is not a missing link — it never *was*.

## PROOF OF ITS KIND

The proof of the inviolability of the Word of God that no evolution from one species to another is possible lies in a well-known fact. The test of a species (admitted by scientists) is the fertility of its offspring. If the children or offspring of parents are fertile, able to reproduce, it is proof positive that the parents were of the same species. Individuals of different species cannot usually interbreed, hence they have no offspring or the offspring is sterile and cannot reproduce. It stops right there.

We refer again to the case of the donkey and the mare which may produce a mule, but it is always sterile, and reproduction stops right there. God said this six thousand years or more ago, "after its kind." Now follow this logic: Without a change of species, (one form into another) there can be no evolution, and without fertility there can be no descendants from parents of a different species. All of this, science has proven and pointed out, and is its own argument against the evolution of lower forms into higher, such as the monkey into man. "After its kind" is God's rule and the insurmountable barrier standing in the way of evolution from lower forms of life to a higher by evolution.

## MANY VARIETIES

We may sum up the findings of science in four words, *mutations but no transmutation.* Varieties within the species are limitless and man has succeeded by selective breeding and scientific means in improving many plants and animals and producing many new varieties: cattle without horns, white turkeys, seedless oranges, and we hope some day "squirt-less" grapefruit. Think of the hundreds of varieties of monkeys, but there is not one human among them. Luther Burbank never developed a rose from a daffodil.

## THE MINK FARM

I have a friend in northern Michigan who is a scientific breeder of mink. Now the wild mink is uniformly a brown color with a bit of white here and there. However, my friend has an almost unbelievable variety of colors among his thousands of mink. Some are jet black, others white, brown, platinum-gray and various other shades. This man Anderson knows his mink. He has a record of ancestry of each mink, the color of its parents and grandparents. He knows exactly what genetic combination will result in certain colors. By an inviolable law of genetics he can produce the color which is most in demand according to the whims of fashion. If he breeds a black male with a platinum female, he can tell what color the "kits" will be. The variations and possibilities are almost unlimited. But now here comes my point. No matter what differences in size, color, temperament or resistances to disease are produced by this genetic selective breeding, he never yet has mated two mink and had them produce a litter of porcupines. They are always *mink*. No, it is ever *after its kind*.

## Spiritual Application

Now why do we go into all this detail? Because it is basic and germane as affecting the matter of our eternal salvation, as well as proving the inspiration of the Bible. Evolution has no place for the creation of man in the image of God as a separate work of God. Therefore, it has no place for the fall of man; and if there is no room for a fall, how then can we account for sin, evil, sickness and death in the world? And if there is no fall, there is no need for a Saviour. The descendants of apes and monkeys don't need a Saviour. If humanity evolved from a lower animal, then the Saviour of the world, the Lord Jesus Christ, was the offspring of a brute instead of having the nature of man. There is no room in the doctrine of the evolution of man from the lower animals, for the virgin birth, the atoning death, the bodily resurrection or the coming again of Jesus Christ. Evolution and the Bible record of the creation of man are incompatible.

## The New Creation

If the truth of the creation of the earth according to Genesis 1 is not true, then the revelation concerning a new spiritual creation too falls to the ground. Paul says: "Therefore if any man be in Christ, he is a new [creation] creature . . ." (II Corinthians 5:17).

What we have said about the plants and animals in the natural, applies also in the spiritual. God said, "Let it bring forth after its kind." This was true of Adam. Of him we read:

> . . . In the day that God created man, in the likeness of God made he him [not in the likeness of an ape];
> Male and female created he them; and blessed them, and called their name Adam, in the day when they were created.
> And Adam lived an hundred and thirty years, and begat a son *in his own likeness, after his image*; and called his name Seth (Genesis 5:1-3).

Notice this law of "like producing like" operated in Adam for he begat a son in his own image. Notice! *In his own image,* and Adam was created in the image of God. When Seth was born, however, Adam was a sinner and according to the law of heredity, Seth was born a little sinner, and that law has never been violated, and all Adam's seed since that day have been born *sinners,* for "like produces like." David said, "Behold, I was shapen in iniquity; and in sin did my mother conceive me" (Psalm 51:5).

Paul says, "For all have sinned, and come short of the glory of God" (Romans 3:23).

For this reason the sinner must be created anew. He needs a second birth. He cannot, by a process of evolution, develop from a sinner into a saint. As there is no room for evolution of the first Adam from an ape, so a "new creature" in Christ Jesus is not an evolution of a sinner into a saint, by the forces of education, reformation, religion, ritual or ordinance. Jesus said *no!* "Ye must be born *anew,* born from *above.*" And the reason? The same reason as in Genesis 1. Like produces like. It must be a new creation. We refer you again to Jesus' words in John 3: "That which is born of the flesh is flesh" (John 3:6).

And that flesh will never evolve into Spirit. That which is flesh is flesh and can never be anything else. And then He adds: ". . . and that which is born of the Spirit is spirit. Marvel not that I said unto thee, Ye must be born again" (John 3:6, 7).

The enemy of our souls, the author of material evolution, is also deceiving men and women concerning the second spiritual creation. He would have us believe that within the natural man there is a germ of goodness, a divine spark, which needs only to be cultivated and educated, and it will develop into sainthood by a gradual evolution. It is the error of spiritual evolution — gaining salvation by training, religion, ritual, good works, ceremonies and ordinances, but Jesus says, "YE MUST BE BORN AGAIN."

Listen as we close with the words of Paul, "For in Christ Jesus neither circumcision availeth any thing, nor uncircumcision, but a *NEW CREATURE*" (Galatians 6:15).

NOT EVOLUTION — BUT CREATION!

## Chapter Eleven

## NOTHING NEW UNDER THE SUN

*And the Lord God formed man of the dust of the
ground, and breathed into his nostrils the breath of
life; and man became a living soul* (Genesis 2:7).

This verse if it means anything at all teaches at least three
things:

1. Man was brought into being by a distinct creative act of
God.

2. His body was molded from dead earth or dust and was
not the result of reproduction by another body or bodies.

3. His soul was the result of God imparting life by His Spirit
and not by the generation of life from another creature.

Adam's body was made from the earth. The word "formed"
in Genesis 2:7 is "yatsar" (pronounced yaw-tsar') in the original
and means "to press into shape." It may also be translated
"molded," as a potter molds the clay into shape. The same
word "yatsar" is also used for the creation of animals and fowl:
"And out of the ground the LORD God formed (molded) every
beast . . . and every fowl . . ." (Genesis 2:19).

### BODIES ALIKE

Since the body of Adam was formed from the same soil as
beasts and birds, they are naturally similar in substance.
Chemically the body of a man consists of essentially the same
elements as the body of a sheep, a bird or a pig. However,
from this it cannot be argued that the one evolved from the
other. It merely establishes the fact that physically all bodies
are taken from the same original stuff. Just because a clay pipe
is made of the same clay as a brick does not prove the pipe

79

evolved from the brick. But chemical elemental structure does not end the similarity of the bodies of animals and man. For there is one general pattern which is common to both. Animals are like man physically in many ways, and seem to be patterned after the same general model, having eyes, ears, hair or feathers, limbs, stomach, mouth, kidneys, liver, heart, etc., etc., etc. These are common both to animals and man. But this does not prove evolution. It only proves that one and the same Creator made them all. The fact that two houses have similar floor plan and design does not prove that one house is the result of an evolution of the other. It only suggests that the two houses were separately designed, independently of each other, but by the same architect. The argument of science in favor of evolution, based on the similarity of physical, physiological and anatomic structure of birds, beasts and man, proves only the same wise Creator, but certainly not evolution.

## Author of Life

The difference between animals and man goes far deeper than a physical variation. It is in the spiritual that animals and man have nothing in common. Man is a spiritual being. He became so by the breath or Spirit of God. ". . . God . . . breathed into his nostrils the breath [spirit] of life; and man became a living soul" (Genesis 2:7).

This sets man forever apart from all the rest of creation. Science itself has given proof that the unique "life" of man cannot be traced to a lower creature. For centuries upon centuries it was believed that life could be produced spontaneously from dead matter. As early as the fourth century before Christ, Aristotle taught as incontrovertible truth the doctrine of abiogenesis. It was not until the nineteenth century when the discoveries of Pasteur definitely proved that there can be no life without antecedent life, that the theory of spontaneous generation was abandoned. Recently experiments to produce life in a test tube from inert substances was revived. Such is the stupidity of human wisdom which rejects the Word of God. Infidelity just will never learn.

## No Transmutation

But while the idea of spontaneous generation has been completely abandoned, the belief in evolution of lower forms of life into higher is being freely taught as a proven fact and avidly accepted by those who reject the Scriptural account. According to modern evolutionists, the organic world consists of a connected chain, beginning with the single cell and ending with man. The change, it is said, comes by adaptation to changing circumstances. As an example our attention is called to the giraffe, living in central Africa where the ground vegetation is often very sparse, and as a result is compelled to feed instead on the foliage of trees. By constantly being compelled to stretch itself to reach the foliage on the trees, both its legs and neck stretched longer and longer so that finally it "evolved" into the ungainly, long-legged, long-necked giraffe. This is referred to as natural adaptation.

The same reasoning in reverse was used to explain the long legs of the crane, herons, and similar birds. It is explained that these beautiful birds dreaded to get their plumage wet and so developed the long legs and necks, not to reach up like a giraffe, but to reach down instead. This too was Darwin's theory, that by a vital adaptability it fostered natural selection. Those animals who did not have long necks to reach high enough for the foliage, ultimately died of starvation, while the long-necked ones survived and resulted in a new species — giraffes having probably started as alligators in the first place. This theory denies the Bible account which definitely states that "God made the beast of the field *after its kind.*"

The facts of nature disprove this theory of natural selection, or survival of the fittest, as applied to the transmutation of species. It is a fact that improvements in a species are the result of "cultivation" and not natural selection. The various superior varieties of a certain species result from careful cultivation, selective breeding, and intelligent cross-pollination. Left alone these superior varieties will not improve but instead will revert to the original strain. Neglected, these strains all revert to the wild. The huge strawberries in my garden, developed by science, all came originally from the little wild berry, and if left alone will soon revert to its original parent again, the little tart strawberry of the woods and fields. How then does it come that evolution would suppose the very opposite — that plants and animals left alone and uncultivated would develop not only into new varieties but actually new species? My good friend, the mink farmer mentioned previously, assures me if all his mink were left to interbreed naturally and undirected, that in a few generations they would all revert to the common brown mink of the wilds and streams.

Let the external influences become once more what they originally were — that is, let culture cease and let it be left to become wild, and the species will lose its different varieties and return to its original type. It is the exact opposite of the theories of evolution. It has been proven that all the varieties of tame pigeons, tumblers, pouters, carriers, fantails, etc., when left alone to interbreed on an isolated island, reverted to the original slate-colored wild pigeon, even regaining the two dark rings about the legs. In the same way, the some odd four thousand varieties of roses, in the absence of cultivation, soon revert back to the simple single wild rose. The naturalist knows that all the different breeds of dogs from the tiny toy Pekingese to the giant Mastiff can be led back to the original ground type — the wolf, fox, or jackal.

Now place these facts over against the teaching of evolutionists with the theory of adaptation to environment and circumstances and natural selection. Take again, for instance, the case of the adaptable giraffe. Because it was constantly standing on tiptoes and stretching its neck to reach its food, it finally developed and evolved into the ungainly long-legged, long-necked clown of the desert. If this theory is true, it certainly suggests some gruesome possibilities for our race. We can imagine the man of the future as a curious looking creature, if this evolution continues. With natural selection and adaptation and continued evolution we may expect various species of men in this world of specialized occupation. We may expect to see humpbacked farmers with enormous muscular bodies, large-headed students with short-sighted eyes, office workers with useless shrunken legs, many-fingered piano players, mail carriers with legs way out of proportion to their bodies, and night-watchmen with bulging eyes as big as saucers. What a gruesome sight a few hundred years from now presents to us. Over against all this stands the immutable Word of God, "everything after its kind." This kind or species is fixed and immutable.

## A FINISHED CREATION

Since God ended His creative work at the close of the sixth day, there has been nothing added. The work was complete and all the changes which have taken place have been within the limits of mutations within the species to which each new variety belongs. This is asserted without apology in the opening verse of Genesis 2: "Thus the heavens and the earth were finished, and all the host of them."

God finished His work. It was completed. He did not merely start it going and then leave it to evolve into something. The work was *finished*. It means to bring to a complete end. There was nothing more to be done, and so God rested from "*All* his work which he had made" (Genesis 2:2).

Since that day, there has been nothing added. There has been no evolution from one finished product to another. Solomon said, "There is nothing new under the sun." Every discovery of man is only the repetition of something God had already placed in creation, and was there when God said it was finished. Every element known to man today was created the moment God spoke the word which brought matter into being. Every atom was potentially present when God finished His creation. It may evidence itself in energy, power, life, heat, or motion, but it was there. And the laws which governed these elements and atoms were fixed and unchangeable. The laws of chemical reaction and combinations were all forever fixed. The laws of life and germination and growth and heredity and genetics have never been altered. When God finished His work, it was done. It was perfect, it was complete. Since that day of which Genesis 2:1 says, "Thus the heavens and the earth were finished" and He rested from creation, nothing has been added; nothing more has been created. No new elements were added because God had forgotten one. Not one atom was overlooked. How different the work of man! He has never yet made a perfect work or machine, but must constantly alter and change it; parts must be added and parts deleted and changed. Man never gets "all the bugs" out of anything he makes. His progress is by trial and error, ever seeking to improve but never reaching perfection. Each year sees a new model of car with new gadgets never thought of before, and again and again the manufacturer must replace the old with something better.

But not so with God's creation. It was complete and perfect, and we read: "And God saw everything that he had made, and, behold, it was very good . . ." (Genesis 1:31).

In the original it reads, "God saw all He had made, and behold — very good." God said, "Very good." It is perfect, complete. But it was not only good in the matter of its elemental constitution, but He placed within this created matter a set of laws, rules, and regulations which would never need revision, alteration or change. Every law of chemistry, physics, heredity, genetics, is fixed and always operates the same way according to a fixed principle under set circumstances. The laws of gravity, evaporation, condensation, adhesion, cohesion, magnetism, osmosis, growth and metabolism of vegetable and animal life, have been operating without change from the beginning of time. And the basic law in creation that there is nothing new under the sun, negates and destroys the entire philosophy of evolution which would teach that a higher can evolve from a lower, and that God's laws are not fixed. For God said of vegetation, "let the herbs and fruit trees bring forth *after its kind.*"

That is a fixed law — "like always produces like," and there is not one speck of evidence science can put forward that one species has ever broken God's law and produced a different kind of offspring than itself. It is all in the realm of the speculative. There may be development and an evolution "within" the confines of each species, but it will always be *after its kind.* The same is true of fish, birds and animals (Genesis 1:21). The whole truth can be summed up in the words of Galatians 6:7, "Be not deceived; God is not mocked: for whatsoever a man soweth, that shall he also reap."

This is the law of creation — "after its kind." Creation, not evolution, is God's answer to all the questions: Who made the world? Where did it come from? When did it begin? and more than that, it also tells us where it is going. And what we said about the old creation is true of the new. Salvation is not an evolution but a *new creation*. Salvation is not a gradual development of a sinner into a saint. It is an immediate creation. The author of spiritual evolution, the Devil, would have us believe that there is in all of us a spark of the divine (a spiritual primordial cell), and all this needs is a fanning of improvement and it will finally burst into the flame of redemption. And so we are taught that all of us have some good in us which only needs cultivation, by education, religion, ethics, church membership, and ceremonies, and then the good in all of us will come out and evolve into a beautiful Christianity.

But God says *no!* There is not a little good spark, a little beginning blob of spiritual protoplasm in all of us. Instead the Word declares:

> The LORD looked down from heaven upon the children of men, to see if there were any that did understand, and seek God.
> They are all gone aside, they are all together become filthy: there is none that doeth good, no, not one (Psalm 14:2, 3).

There is God's answer to the spiritual counterpart of evolution. God began it with nothing and must begin the new creation in the same way — not evolution but a *new creation*.

> Jesus answered and said unto him, Verily, verily, I say unto thee, Except a man be born again, he cannot see the kingdom of God (John 3:3).

*Chapter Twelve*

# AFTER ITS KIND

The Bible claims that the universe came into being by a creative act of Almighty God. He is the great first cause, and His Word is the only authentic and reasonable explanation for the existence of the universe, including this earth and everything upon it. David says in Psalm 33:6 — "By the word of the LORD were the heavens made; and all the host of them by the breath of his mouth."

This verse tells us it was a triune God who created the heavens. God made it all by His Son Jesus Christ who was the eternal Word. By this Word "all things were made." And the Holy Spirit too was operative in this creation, for He made them by "the breath of his mouth." The word "breath" is *ruach* in the original and is the same word translated "spirit" in other places.

The original creation was, according to the Bible, a single immediate act and not a prolonged evolutionary process, for David says in Psalm 33:9, "For he spake, and it was done; he commanded, and it stood fast."

But vain man is quite unwilling to accept God's own account of creation and seeks in a thousand ways to get rid of God. Today the theories of evolution are generally accepted even by people who still claim to believe the Bible. Recently in a dozen magazines the story of the evolution of man from a primordial cell was boldly and graphically pictured, step by step without one shred of substantiating facts or even an apology. In our children's books of nature, artistic charts and diagrams depict the history of man beginning with a bit of protoplasm through the successive stages of worm, fish, fowl, mammal, monkey, to man, without one single proven fact. In many schools, evolution is taught and accepted as fact while the Bible is banned! And all

86

this in the face of the unmet challenge to produce one single proven instance of evolution from a lower form of life to a higher one. There has never, there can never, be any change by evolutionary processes from one "kind" of creature to another. God's Word still stands: "Let the earth bring forth . . . after its kind."

*After its kind! After its kind!* While scores of theories once considered scientific have come and gone, God's Word spoken over six thousand years ago still stands: *after its kind.* That one statement, "after its kind," is the obstacle which evolution has never been able to hurdle. There it stands, immovable, unanswerable. Give one exception to the law, "Let it produce after its kind." Prove one single instance, just one, where peaches grew on an apple tree, where a dog gave birth to kittens, where ducks hatched from chicken eggs, and I will throw my Bible away.

## THE PILTDOWN MAN

In spite of all the errors and mistakes of the evolution exponents, however, the deception still persists. What folly to place a pile of bones and fossils against the plain teachings of the Book. Again and again, these great discoveries were proven false, in some instances gigantic hoaxes. Consider one of the more recent examples, "the Piltdown Man." For forty years the world of scientists was fooled by the so-called Piltdown Man, *discovered* by Charles Dawson in the south of England and long called "Eoranthropus" (dawn man), and reputed to be from 100,000 to 500,000 years old! The Smithsonian Institution of Washington gives details of the deception in "The Great Piltdown Hoax."

> Careful "detective" work done by Dr. J. S. Weiner, and others, revealed that "the lower jaw and the canine tooth are actually those of a modern anthropoid ape, deliberately altered (filed down by a joker) so as to resemble fossil specimens." The faker had cunningly "fossilized" the jaw and teeth by staining them a mahogany color with an iron salt and bichromate!

If "experts" and "scientists" can be so easily fooled by a fraudulent fossil, will they not do as badly in trying to interpret the whole history of creation from bones, fossils, and unproven theories?

No Christian is fooled by believing the Bible, and no discerning believer in the Word of God would ever fall for such a hoax. Yet we are considered stupid by the intellectual evolution exponents. We are considered gullible and simple-minded to believe that the Bible record of creation is literally true, instead of believing the fantastic theory of spontaneous generation. We are considered stupid because we just accept the Word of God by faith, even though we are unable to explain why. But is it any more stupid to believe, "In the beginning God created," than to believe that matter always was? If you ask me where God came from, I would simply ask, "Where did matter come from?" Which is easier to believe, that an intelligent, all-wise Being created matter, or that the universe always was, without explanation? Very true, if we say God made the worlds, we can ask the question, "But who made God?" But even if we could prove that someone else made God, then we are still faced with the question, "Who made that someone, who made that God?" And having answered that question, we are faced with the next one, "Who made that someone who made that someone who made that God?" So we can go on and on into infinity. Since evolution deals with time and matter it simply cannot answer the question of ultimate origin, but faith comes to rest on the same rock of Genesis 1:1, "In the beginning God created the heaven and the earth."

## WHAT IS TIME?

How foolish it is, therefore, to try and reach the beginning of eternity, for eternity has no beginning. It is impossible for the human mind to imagine a past eternity. We do not even understand time. Have you ever asked yourself, "What is *time*?" Now think a moment. Tell me, what is it? How long is time? Really? The ticking of the clock is merely a measurement of time. How was eternity measured before there was time? Why does time measure a creature's life and cause one to last for long periods of time and another to exist just for a few hours of time? Why does an insect live a few hours and a cat about ten to fifteen years, some birds only a few years, a lion thirty years, a crow one hundred years and man eighty years? What is there about time which sets the years of our lives? Time is made up of moments and each fraction of a moment is a part of time. Time is therefore only an infinitesimally brief moment as compared with eternity. And science tells us nothing about eternity but is confined entirely to a study of time.

With every tick a "moment" enters your life, a stranger from eternity casts a glance at you, and is gone before you can stretch out your hand to grasp it. What will the next bring to you? Failure of the heart's action, perhaps, and in the one after, you *are* no more! You *were!* You are to your dear ones now only a memory. Or, the next moment the bell rings! The postman! A telegram! You read it. It tells of the death of one of your dearest; or perhaps of ruin, disgrace, misfortune, to yourself or your family — for misfortune lies in wait for us. Nearer and nearer comes the last moment of all; a long or short death struggle, and the doctor says, "It is all over." Your family bursts into tears, and they kiss the pale form which until now was you; but you have left forever the earth, where time flowed on like a river; you are there where the eons roll onward in God, like shoreless and fathomless oceans — the true time of which ours is only an image and an outflow. Everything in this world happens in time. Men are born and die "in the fulness of time." "And it came to pass," say the Scriptures. Every moment that passes belongs to past time — irreclaimable, unattainable, whether great, important, blissful, sorrowful, or tedious. Time is but a pause between the two abysses of a beginningless and an endless eternity, and your sojourn is but a tiny segment of the tiny segment of time. And when our "time" is up, as it has been for other generations now gone and will be for everyone else, then what? For God has said, "It is appointed unto men once to die, but after this the judgment" (Hebrews 9:27). Solomon says that "man goeth to his long home. . . . Then shall the dust return to the earth . . . and the spirit shall return unto God who gave it" (Ecclesiastes 12:5, 7).

## THEN WHAT?

Then what? Tell us, ye men of science. After this life then what? You evolutionists who can prate so volubly about our origin, can you tell us about our future destiny? What about the future? What about eternity? You who speak so positively on where we came from, tell us, where are we going? Tell us if you can. . . .

Mocking silence, embarrassing silence, is the answer of science and evolution. But we must have an answer! Eternity will, unlike time, never end. What about .eternity? Where I came from is of little importance to me, now that I face a future eternity. But man has no answer and so I must turn to the Word of God for my only answer. The only source of information concerning my future is the Bible. But if the Bible cannot be accepted when it tells where we came from, then how can I trust it when it tells me where I am going? Until evolution can prove where we came from and tell us where we are going, we shall stick by the Book which says about the past, "In the beginning God created" man in his own image; and of the future, "it is appointed unto men once to die, but after this the judgment." I shall believe the One who said, "I am Alpha and Omega, the beginning and the end, the first and the last" (Revelation 22:13).

## THE END OF EVOLUTION

It is God's Word against man's infidelity. It is the old, old story of the Garden of Eden. God had said, "Ye shall surely die." The Devil said, "Ye shall *not* surely die." It was the word of God against the word of the creature. The result we all know was death and the curse and Hell, and the same is true today. Either one believes God's Word or he denies it, and upon this hangs man's eternal destiny, for Jesus Himself says: "He that believeth on him is not condemned: but he that believeth not is condemned already, because he hath not believed in the name of the only begotten Son of God" (John 3:18).

To believe on Jesus, it is imperative that you believe the record of the creation of man in the image of God as recorded in Genesis 1:27. Let me repeat that statement. You cannot believe in Jesus Christ if you reject the account of man's creation in the image of God in Genesis, for Jesus Himself places His stamp of approval on the record. Both Matthew and Mark record Jesus' quoting of Genesis 1:27,

> . . . Have ye not read, that he which made them [man and woman] at the beginning made them male and female (Matthew 19:4).
>
> But from the beginning of the creation God made them male and female (Mark 10:6).

Jesus says man's origin in the *beginning* was a creative act of God, not after a long evolutionary period. He made them in the beginning. If then evolution is correct and the first man evolved from a lower animal, then Jesus was mistaken. And this is the damning result of the now widely accepted theory of the organic evolution of man from a lower animal; it destroys Jesus as the perfect Saviour, and with it goes God's entire plan of redemption.

That is why, at the risk of criticism, ridicule and scoffing, we are writing this book, to counteract, refute, deny, condemn, and challenge this damning error which is being freely taught in our institutions of learning and even defended in religious circles. The teaching of man's origin from an ape, even theistic evolution, will result in a degeneration which only the judgment of God will bring to an end. Think of the natural results of what is taught. Teach men the Bible truth of man's dignified origin, and it will create a sense of desire to again become in the image of God. Teach man he is descended from the beasts, and he will soon begin to act like a beast. I do not doubt that the tremendous upsurge in crime, sadism, sexuality, and bestial acts can be directly traced to the teaching of evolution. It destroys every sense of responsibility to God.

Teach man as the Bible does that, though created in the image of God, the race fell down — not evolved upward — and needs a Saviour, and that the man Christ Jesus is that Saviour, the Son of God — not the son of an ape, and there is hope for man.

One reason so many young people are confused is because they are told that no intelligent person believes the Bible story of creation any more, or as one person wrote, "Every educated person today believes in evolution." That is the Devil's lie, the same lie he told Eve — that God's Word was not true.

We believe the time has come to speak out on this matter. It is a sad commentary on the virility, or rather the lack of the virility of modern Christendom, that this error has been propagated with such a minimum of opposition and denial from our Christian platforms and pulpits. We are to blame for letting this baseless denial of God's Word gain such wide acceptance, by our silence, caused I am afraid by our fear of being called old-fashioned, ignorant, and unscientific. There is no excuse for this inferiority complex. Let us tell our young people that the evolution of man from a lower animal is a fable, a myth, an unproven and unprovable theory. Tell them the Word of God is true and its teachings need no apologies. If believing the creation account of Genesis is a sign of ignorance, then Moses, David, Paul, and Jesus were ignoramuses. Modern scholarship prates about the dignity of man and then debases him by tracing his ancestry to a most undignified chimpanzee. Which is more dignified? God's record or man's speculation? Where will you take your stand? It will determine your eternal destiny. If you do not believe the record of Genesis, you cannot be saved, for Jesus said:

> For had ye believed Moses, ye would have believed me: for he wrote of me.
> But if ye believe not his [Moses'] writings, how shall ye believe my words? (John 5:46, 47).

## Chapter Thirteen

## THE TWO CREATIONS

*For in Christ Jesus neither circumcision availeth any
thing, nor uncircumcision, but a new creature (Galatians
6:15).*

The believer is called a new "creation." The same word is
used for the creation of the universe and the new birth by
which a sinner becomes a saint. In the record of the original
material creation as recorded in Genesis, we have therefore in
shadow and type also a picture of the spiritual creation, the new
birth and development of the believer. We must remember that
the Bible was written primarily for the purpose of revealing
the plan of redemption. While all the Bible is infallible and it
records a great deal of history, geography, geology and other
related sciences, these are incidental to the main purpose of the
book—the revelation of Jesus Christ as the Saviour of the world.
This is true of every verse in the Bible. It is true of the first
chapter with which the Bible opens, "In the beginning God created the heaven and the earth."

This opening verse, while it records for us the origin of this
material universe, is nevertheless an introduction to another
revelation concerning the spiritual *new creation*. While we believe the record of creation and the first three chapters of the
Bible to be a literal account, we must not forget that it was
meant to teach a spiritual lesson, the lesson of another creation, as mysterious and miraculous as the other.

### NOT FOR CURIOSITY

The story of creation in Genesis was not given to satisfy our
curiosity or to explain in detail all about the origin of the uni-

verse. If that had been God's purpose, He would have gone into much greater detail and devoted much more space to the matter of when and how God made all things. How we would like to know, but God has apparently withheld the details of the material creation, lest we should become so occupied with it that we miss the spiritual lesson. Redemption is the theme of the Bible, and all these questions concerning the beginnings of things are quite secondary to this redemptive revelation. "What shall it profit a man if he gain the whole world?" says Jesus. If gaining the whole world cannot profit, then simply knowing about this whole world would be of still less profit, if in gaining that knowledge he lose his own soul.

## BIBLE IS SILENT

The Bible, therefore, is completely silent on the details concerning the original creation, except for the final statement, "In the beginning God created." He gives us only enough information which, in the light of subsequent revelation, is needed to be saved. Man, however, is not inclined to seek the spiritual teaching of the narrative, but wants to pry back into the unknown. He wants to know about the past, the irrevocable past, and neglects the all-important future. God's program is just the opposite. God passes by the past in a couple of verses and spends the rest of the time in trying to interest us in the future.

This spiritual lesson is stamped unmistakably on the opening verses of the Bible. The first verse tells us of a perfect creation. But sin entered and brought the curse of death. We remind you once more that the silence between the first and second verses of Genesis is indicative. In verse one a perfect creation; Isaiah tells us that the earth was not made void, waste, dark and frozen. Yet in the second verse we read: "And the earth was [became] without form [waste], and void; and darkness was upon the face of the deep" (Genesis 1:2).

This is the Bible picture of man as a result of his fall. When man sinned he was not just wounded and therefore needs some doctoring up; he was not just sick and needs the medicine of culture, training, education, and determination to fix him up. Ah, no! The sinner "died," broke with his God, and is lost, helpless and undone. The sinner without Christ is a total wreck. Nothing he can do has any merit with God. The Bible is very clear on this. The Bible says that,

> . . . without faith it is impossible to please him [God] (Hebrews 11:6).
> . . . they that are in the flesh cannot please God (Romans 8:8).
> . . . all our righteousnesses are as filthy rags (Isaiah 64:6).

The modern prattling about the dignity of human nature and the spark of the divine is just a clever deception of the enemy of our souls. Man through sin is graphically pictured by the scene of ruin and darkness as we see the earth in Genesis 1:2, waste, void, under darkness. Without outside intervention it would have remained thus forever. There were no latent residential forces within this dead matter which could be awakened by anything within itself. There were not some residual sleeping primordial germs which could somehow awaken themselves and begin the chain of evolution which ultimately blossomed forth in a monkey who became father to a man. This earth under the curse of God was dead, lifeless, helpless. It was waste and void and without light; and without light there could be no life.

### SPIRITUAL APPLICATION

This is the teaching of the Bible concerning the first creation. Created in perfection by God, but ruined by sin, it was a complete loss. But the very hopeless condition was the setting for a grand exhibition of the Creator's power in bringing life out of death, and something out of nothing. Before the sinner, therefore, can become a new creation, he must be reduced to nothing, for the very word, "creation," in its strictest sense means to produce out of nothing. As long as the sinner imagines he can do anything to merit, earn, or deserve salvation, he is hopeless. As long as the sinner imagines he can help God in the least, lift one little finger in behalf of his salvation, he cannot be saved. As long as the sinner imagines that there is just a little goodness in himself, something which God will accept as a claim to his salvation, he cannot be saved. The Bible is crystal-clear on this.

This is the meaning of "conviction." Jesus said of the Holy Spirit that when He is come He will "reprove the world of sin, and of righteousness, and of judgment" (John 16:8). The word translated "reprove" means to "convict" and is so translated in the revised version. The word, "convict," means to pronounce guilty (according to Webster). The first work of the Holy Spirit upon the sinner is to prove him guilty, strip him of every excuse. The Spirit first convicts the sinner, proves his guilt, and then offers salvation. But until the sinner admits his guilt he cannot be saved. Christ Jesus came to die for sinners. Good people cannot be saved — only sinners. The Bible says, "there is none good, no not one," and until a man is willing to acknowledge his utter worthlessness he is still lost. We often sing the Scriptural hymn, but I wonder how much of it we believe:

> Nothing in my hand I bring,
> Simply to Thy Cross I cling.

When God creates a new thing, He begins with nothing. It was so in the beginning of the world: "In the beginning God created the heaven and the earth." He began with only Himself — nothing else. And this is just as true of the new creation; it must be all the work of God.

But this original creation in Genesis 1:1 was ruined by the sin of Satan, and so God begins to restore this creation. It began with the creation of light. It was completed at the sabbath of rest. This, too, is a picture of the spiritual new creation. Once man was created in the image of God. He fell and he, too, like the world in Genesis 1:2, became waste (fruitless) and void (utterly worthless) and under darkness (blinded by sin). The ruin was complete and then God began to work. It was first the brooding of the Spirit of God upon this dead mass: ". . . And the Spirit of God moved upon the face of the waters" (Genesis 1:2).

Salvation is of the Lord. It begins with God because it is a new creation. As in the old creation, so in the new. When a sinner awakens to his need of salvation it is already the work of the Holy Spirit. When a sinner becomes conscious of his guilt and sin, and conviction grips his soul, it is because the Holy Spirit has awakened within him this conviction. Then follows light; the sinner sees his true condition. Remember, the world was waste, void, and plunged in darkness. The condition of the earth was invisible, it was hidden in darkness. But when God said, "Let there be light," it revealed the awful mess, the terrible scene of chaos and judgment. It brought to light a world of ruin, barrenness and hopelessness. That was the first thing the creation of light on the first day revealed.

This is paralleled by the experience of the sinner. The first evidence of the brooding work of the Holy Spirit is a conviction of sin. This is produced by the light of the Word of God revealing to the lost soul the awfulness and reality, nature and judgment of sin. Though this conviction of sin in conversion may or may not be accompanied by visible emotional evidences, conviction of sin is absolutely necessary. All of which demonstrates that God first reduces what He intends to create to *nothing*. Before the sinner can receive life, he must be dead.

## THE GRAIN OF WHEAT

Jesus in John 12 enunciated this principle, in His answer to the Greeks who came with the question, "Sir, we would see Jesus." Jesus answered them: ". . . Except a corn of wheat fall into the ground and die, it abideth alone: but if it die, it bringeth forth much fruit" (John 12:24).

The first interpretation, of course, is that only by the death of the Lord Jesus on the Cross can He become the Saviour. But we may also make the application to the sinner who must die to self before he can receive life. But once the sinner has renounced all claim to God's mercy and by the light of the Holy Spirit upon the Word of God he is saved, then "he who began a good work will continue to accomplish it until the day of Jesus Christ." In our coming messages we shall trace the seven steps in the salvation process beginning with conversion and resulting in the ultimate victory of the Christian believer. This growth in grace, this development of our spiritual life, also called practical sanctification, is clearly revealed in type in the seven days of creation in Genesis 1. May I suggest and strongly urge that before going on you memorize thoroughly the seven days of creation in their order. It will be of immeasurable help in appreciating the coming messages as we apply the record of the original creation to our spiritual new birth and subsequent growth to the full maturity of Christian experience. The seven days of creation are as follows:

1. First day, *light;* beginning of the work of the Holy Spirit resulting in conviction and conversion.

2. Separation of waters on the earth and above the earth; picture of the separated walk of the believer.

3. Creation of vegetation and fruit trees on earth; a picture of the fruit in the life of the believer as an evidence of the new life.

4. Creation of sun, moon and stars – light bearers; picturing our testimony and shining for Christ.

5. Fish and fowl produced; picture of victory over the pull of the earth, and the victorious Christian life.

6. Creation of cattle and man; speaking of service and formation into the image of God.

7. Perfect peace and rest; the ultimate goal of the new creature.

Memorize these seven days in the order in which they occur and then grade yourself, if you are a Christian, on how far you have progressed in your Christian growth. And if you are not saved, you are still in darkness, dead in trespasses and in sins. If anything you have read has awakened within you a sense of need, a consciousness of your lost condition, then open your heart to the Holy Spirit and experience the transforming power of the Word of God when He says, "Let there be light."

It is so simple. God offers you salvation – you must receive it.

1. God has done His part – John 3:16.

2. Now it's up to you – John 1:12.

*Chapter Fourteen*

# COME OUT FROM AMONG THEM

Two eminent, highly educated scientists were teachers in the same college and also happened to live on the same street and, of all things, next door to each other. They were close friends in their scientific fields, and yet in another sense they were total strangers, for the one was a devout, Bible-believing Christian, while the other was an avowed atheist and rejected the Bible record of creation as fantastic and scientifically untenable. It was a strange relationship, for while they had much in common in the intellectual field, they were at complete odds in the spiritual realm. Both were brilliant men, keen thinkers, yet the two could scarcely be farther apart on the scientific question of the origin of the universe. The Christian was greatly exercised about his colleague's unbelief and sought in every way to show him the folly of his position, all the while realizing his associate needed to have his spiritual eyes opened first of all. Many a serious discussion ended nowhere. The infidel was a real gentleman and did not resent his friend's attempts to convert him, but always ended up with, "Your belief in God and creation doesn't make sense. I believe that the whole world and everything in it just evolved through inherent residential forces."

Finally the Christian educator conceived an idea. He ordered a beautiful plastic globe of the world to be made by an expert who was known to both the scientists. He created a beautiful globe, made to exact scale, with all the continents, seas, islands and mountains in proper perspective in perfect relief. The blue seas were depressed, the brown continental areas elevated, and the mountain ranges covered with white snows, towering still higher. The globe showed all the lakes, seas and rivers in their proper relations. He made it flattened at the poles as science tells us it is. Then it was mounted on its stand, tilted at just the scientific degree of the earth's inclined axis. It was a work of precision and art. Upon completion the Christian professor placed it in the center of his study upon a stand and then called up his infidel friend to come over for a visit.

As the unbelieving scientist entered the room, the first thing he saw was, of course, the globe. Awed by its beauty he stepped up to it, and in speechless admiration studied its details, perfect contour, adherence to fact and scale, and finally exclaimed, "Who in the world made that beautiful thing for you?"

His friend smiled and said, "No one."

"Now quit joking," replied the friend. "Answer me, who made that for you?"

And again the answer, "No one."

"But where did you get it?"

"Nowhere," was the reply. "This little insignificant replica of the earth just — just — well, it just happened! It may have started from a blob of proto — —"

"Stop! Stop!" said the friend. "You are making a fool out of me. I will be a fool no longer. You win. I see it all now."

Now why couldn't the man see this as he looked at a universe ten billion times more wonderful than a plastic globe? Because he was blind spiritually. He needed to have his spiritual sight given him. He needed to be born again. Jesus said, "Except a man be born again, he cannot see . . ." (John 3:3).

And so as we study the record of the creation of the earth, it is only to illustrate the spiritual new creation. For only "if a man be in Christ is he a new creation." So we refer you to two verses of Scripture widely separated but closely related.

> In the beginning God created the heaven and the earth (Genesis 1:1).
> Therefore if any man be in Christ, he is a new creation (II Corinthians 5:17).

The Bible mentions two creations, a material creation and a spiritual creation. The two works of God, though separate events, are closely related. The material creation is an almost perfect picture of the new and the spiritual creation. For this reason the New Testament speaks of the believer as a *new creation*. The first verse of Genesis tells us of the old creation as it came from the hand of God, good and perfect and beautiful. Then sin came through Satan and left it waste and void and without form. It remained so until the Spirit of the living God began to brood upon the lifeless waste, until it resulted in the bursting forth of light on the first day of the re-creation. This is a perfect picture of the experience of the race. God created man upright in His own image and placed him in a beautiful Garden. But here, too, Satan entered and brought ruin and death upon Adam and Eve and upon the whole race. His condition was utterly hopeless except for one thing. God began to work, and as the Spirit of God moved upon the lifeless chaos of the deep, imparting warmth, the ice began to melt. So, too, man was left helpless in himself. The sinner is dead in sin and cannot move a finger toward his own salvation.

Then the ministry of the Holy Spirit began, the same Spirit who brooded upon the face of the deep. The first sense of need on the part of the sinner is already the work of the Holy Spirit. Man was not so smart that he figured out by himself that he needed to be saved, but the moment the sinner realizes his need of a Saviour, it is already the work of the Holy Spirit. It is He who began brooding upon the face of the deep. This brooding in Genesis 1:2 points to the conviction of the sinner by the Spirit of God. Jesus said of Him, "And when he is come, he will reprove [convict] the world of sin, and of righteousness, and of judgment" (John 16:8).

Do you, my friend, know of what I am speaking? There comes a time in the life of the sinner who is to be saved, when he becomes conscious of his sin. We call it conviction. How well I remember when God's Spirit began brooding over my dead soul early in life. As the result of the teaching of godly parents and some powerful, old-fashioned preaching, during some great crisis or the death of a loved one, I was disturbed and convicted and greatly concerned about my soul. I remember instances early in my life. But it was not until I was thirty-one years old that

I heard the Word of God, "Let there be light, and there was light." I had heard the Word over and over again, and then one day I really *heard it*. After years of brooding of the Spirit, God said, "Let there be light." The darkness disappeared and the light broke through, and for the first time I saw from the WORD that my sins were all borne by the Lord Jesus Christ on the cross, and I could sing from my heart for the first time in my life:

> O happy day that fixed my choice
>   On Thee, my Saviour and my God!
> Well may this glowing heart rejoice,
>   And tell its raptures all abroad.
>
> 'Tis done, the great transaction's done;
>   I am my Lord's, and He is mine;
> He drew me, and I followed on,
>   Charmed to confess the voice divine.
>
> Happy day, happy day, When Jesus washed my sins away!
>   He taught me how to watch and pray,
> And live rejoicing ev'ry day;
>   Happy day, happy day, When Jesus washed my sins away!

Before noticing the next step in the new creation, now begun, let me just remind you that it is all of grace. It was the work of the Holy Spirit, and by the Word of God. Regeneration is the work of the Holy Spirit, and is always accomplished by the WORD of God. God said, "Let there be light." Nothing happens without His Word. Peter tells us in the first chapter of his first epistle: "Being born again, not of corruptible seed, but of incorruptible, by the WORD of God, which liveth and abideth forever" (I Peter 1:23).

You are saved *only* by accepting the promise of God by faith, wholly apart from your goodness or your works.

> He that believeth on the Son of God [and He is the Word of God] hath the witness in himself: he that believeth not God hath made him a liar; because he believeth not the record that God gave of his Son.
> And this is the record, that God hath *given* to us eternal life, and this life is in his Son (I John 5:10, 11).

## THE SECOND DAY

The first day is but the beginning of a week of creation. Seven days elapse before the work begun here is completed. Too many

Christians imagine that once they have believed on the Lord
and have been saved, that this is the end of their salvation, but
it is just the beginning. After the first day comes a second, and
after the second a third, and so on. But the third cannot come
before the second, or the second before the first. The *order* is
as important as the *fact* of each new day. And so the new-born
Christian is taught that now having been saved by grace, the
next step in his Christian growth is *separation*. Let us read the
record. Genesis 1:6-8:

> And God said, Let there be a firmament in the midst
> of the waters, and let it divide the waters from the
> waters.
> And God made the firmament, and divided the waters
> which were under the firmament from the waters which
> were above the firmament: and it was so.
> And God called the firmament HEAVEN. And the
> evening and the morning were the second day.

*Separation!* How little Christians in general know of separation, the second step in salvation. And until we have learned
the lesson of separation on day number two, we cannot go on to
bearing fruit on day number three, or letting our light shine on
day number four. Until you lead a separated life as a believer,
you cannot bear fruit or be a testimony for Christ, much less
experience the victory which the creation of fish and birds teaches
us on the fifth day. How clearly the Word speaks concerning
separation. We hear much about integration today, but very
little of separation. Listen to Paul in Colossians 3:1, 2 —

> If ye then be risen with Christ, seek those things which
> are above . . .
> Set your affection on things above, not on things on
> the earth (Colossians 3:1, 2).

Or listen to Paul again in Romans 12:1, 2, where he says:

> I beseech you therefore, brethren, by the mercies of
> God, that ye present your bodies a living sacrifice, holy,
> acceptable unto God . . .
> And be *not conformed to this world;* but be ye trans-
> formed by the renewing of your mind, that ye may prove
> what is that good, and acceptable, and perfect, will of
> God (Romans 12:1, 2).

How little Christians seem to sense the importance of a life
of separation and non-conformity to the world. The greatest

obstacle to the winning of souls is this, that the sinner so often looks at others who profess to be Christians, and points out their worldly practices and attitude and says, "If so and so is a Christian, then I want none of it." As long as professing Christians continue to copy the fashions of the world, and frequent worldly places and indulge in worldly practices, it will be increasingly difficult to win souls for Christ. The world says pluck your eyebrows till your face looks as bare as a sand dune; Christians pluck their eyebrows and discolor their lips until they look like comedians. Fashion decrees that fingernails shall be painted till they are the color of a corpse and look more like bird claws than fingernails, and Christians follow. And don't think the world does not notice the inconsistency. Even the world expects more of us because we profess to be Christians. And some of you Christian men who take that social drink, play a sociable game in the reeking, smoking den, and tell your suggestive parlor stories, do you really expect ever to lead a soul to Christ? The world soon sees through our shallow, religious veneer, and sits in judgment upon us.

A popular young man in social circles was wonderfully converted during a series of evangelistic meetings, but never having had the background of a spiritual environment, he knew nothing of separation. So when the night for the social club meeting came, he prepared as usual to meet with his buddies at the club. It was a worldly organization, and the members spent most of their time in playing cards, gambling, drinking, and telling questionable stories. When this newly converted young man whom we shall call Joe, entered the clubhouse, he was greeted with an unusual welcome. Said one of his pals, "Well, Joe, boy, am I glad to see you, and to know that what we heard about you was not true at all." Joe was confused and said, "What is this all about anyway? What did you hear?" The reply was, "Why, we heard you had been to that revival meeting and had gotten religion, and were converted. We are so glad to find out it isn't true." Joe was speechless for a moment, and then said, "But it is true. I was at that meeting, and I was converted. It is true." The answer he received to this testimony went straight to his heart. They said, "You say you have been converted — then what are you doing here tonight?"

Friend, does the world know you are a Christian? What estimate do your associates in business and society have of your profession? It is not your testimony at prayer meeting alone, it is not your conduct in church, but what you are when you are among worldly, unconverted people that determines what you really have within you.

## Chapter Fifteen

## BORN TO REPRODUCE

*And God said, Let the waters under the heaven be gathered together unto one place, and let the dry land appear: and it was so.*

*And God called the dry land Earth; and the gathering together of the waters called he Seas: and God saw that it was good.*

*And God said, Let the earth bring forth grass, the herb yielding seed, and the fruit tree yielding fruit after his kind, whose seed is in itself, upon the earth: and it was so.*

*And the earth brought forth grass, and herb yielding seed after his kind, and the tree yielding fruit, whose seed was in itself, after his kind: and God saw that it was good.*

*And the evening and the morning were the third day (Genesis 1:9-13).*

In the previous chapter we have studied the spiritual significance of the first two days of creation as recorded in the first chapter of Genesis. God found man in ruin and darkness as described in the second verse of Genesis 1. Then the Holy Spirit began His brooding work of conviction until the day when God said, "Let there be light." Since Paul calls those who are in Christ "new creations," we pointed out that salvation begins also with the convicting power and influence of the Holy Spirit, until the time when God's Word has its effect in opening the eyes of the blind sinner and the darkness of doubt disappears and the light of the knowledge of salvation shines through. Then followed the second day immediately, the day of *separation*. God divided the waters above in the heavens, from the waters beneath upon the earth. Once the believer is saved, God requires a separated walk before the world and only after he has learned the path of separation is he ready to go into the next experience of growth in grace; namely, the third day of fruit-bearing.

## THE FRUIT OF THE CHRISTIAN

On this third day God caused first of all the dry land to appear, and then on that dry land herbs and trees sprang up. But the part in this day that must be emphasized is that each one of these plants contained within itself the potentialities of bearing fruit *after his kind*. And so we call the third day, the day of *fruit-bearing*. Again and again God says of this vegetation on the third day that its seed was in itself after *his kind*. Again and again God says of the subsequent creation of fish, birds and animals and man, "Be fruitful and fill the earth. Bring forth after your kind." So too in the spiritual realm the Christian, once he has been saved and separated, is next commanded and expected to become fruitful.

Now what is the fruit of the believer? Many I am sure would answer and say, it is love, joy, peace, etc., as given in Galatians 5. But these are the fruit of the Spirit, for "the fruit of the Spirit is love, joy, peace, longsuffering, gentleness, goodness, faith, meekness, temperance" (Galatians 5:22, 23). But the fruit of the believer is quite another thing. You will see this immediately by referring to this third day of creation. The fruit of the herbs was more herbs of the same kind, and the fruit of the trees whose seed was in itself was more trees of its own kind. God laid down a rule which cannot be broken that "like produces like." Everything brings forth *after his kind*. You do not gather figs from grapevines, nor do you harvest barley from wheat seed. A horse never gives birth to a calf and a cow never has a colt. No dog ever had kittens, and no cat ever had puppies; nor can you hatch ducklings from chicken eggs. God laid down the law that everything brings forth *after its kind*. There is no transmutation of the species.

## IN THE SPIRITUAL

The same is true in men. Colored parents do not have white offspring and Dutch parents never have Irish children. Neither do sinners ever beget saints. The fruit is like the tree. And so the Lord Jesus Christ says, "That which is born of the flesh is flesh, and that which is born of the Spirit is Spirit." *After its kind!* And God expects the Christian to reproduce *his kind*. The fruit of the believer then is *other believers*. We are to be spiritual fathers and mothers begetting others for the Lord Jesus and winning souls for Him. The fruit of the believer is more believers. How clearly Solomon puts it in Proverbs 11:30, "The fruit of the righteous is a *tree of life;* and he that winneth souls is wise."

The fruit of the righteous is a tree of life. Not merely a fruit off the tree, but within it another tree again filled with fruit representing more trees. Here is the figure. The believer is a tree, and in that tree is the seed in each fruit for another tree and in each tree there is fruit for more trees. The seed is in itself. The third day then is the day of reproduction. God has so ordered that the creation shall not be made extinct by the failure to reproduce. In each new plant or animal or child is the seed for perpetuating the species. And all nature obeys God's command to *multiply* and bring forth its kind. The herbs scatter their seeds. The tumbleweed lets the wind blow it across the fields to scatter its seed to produce its kind. The cockle burr grasps the hair of the fleeing rabbit or pursuing dog or the clothing of the hunter or farmer that it may be carried far away, there to sow its seed and obey God's command to multiply and bring forth its kind. The birds never disobey God's command. When spring comes they build a cunning nest and lay there the seed of another generation, and carefully incubate it in obedience to God's command. The animals never refuse to reproduce their kind. They never refuse to heed that call and instinct within them to perpetuate their kind.

## BIRTH CONTROL

Only man of all God's creatures, the most intelligent creature on earth originally created in the image of God, refuses to obey God. He alone of all God's creatures has invented "birth control" and practices "race suicide." As a physician I could give you some alarming facts, but I am interested now primarily not in this evil in the natural realm but in the spiritual realm. The curse of modern Christendom is spiritual birth control, the refusal of Christians to be soul winners and to be fruitful and multiply and reproduce their kind. We are so selfish in our search for our own ease and enjoyment that we have no time to permit the Holy Spirit of God to fertilize and impregnate us so we may be spiritual fathers and mothers. Yet that is why God saved you — that you might be the means of saving others. Paul longed to "apprehend that for which he had been apprehended of Christ Jesus" (Philippians 3:12).

Oh, Christian, is your spiritual life barren of fruit? Have you no precious souls to present to Him who gave you eternal life? Have you refused to be a soul winner? Have you shirked the responsibility of spiritual parenthood? Oh then, cry to God to make you a soul winner. Unless you do, you can never go into the fourth day of creation and be a shining star for Him in this dark world.

## THE SEED IS IN YOU

Do not say that you cannot be a soul winner and a fruit-bearer, for God said, "The seed is in itself." It is a physiological fact that in a newborn girl baby all the seed for the coming generation is present even before birth in its mysteriously formed seed pod. The ova which when later fertilized will produce another human being are all there. They only await development at maturity and fertilization. In every believer God has placed the seed of more believers. All you need to do is grow to maturity by feeding on His Word and become fertile by submitting yourself to the Holy Spirit. Yield yourself and your talents, time and will to Him, and you can become a soul winner and a fruit-bearer for Christ. "The fruit of the righteous is a tree of life; and he that winneth souls is wise" (Proverbs 11:30).

## THE FOURTH DAY

If you have a passion for souls, you will be a testimony for the Lord Jesus Christ. And so the fourth day of creation follows the third. Here is the record of the fourth day as given in Genesis 1:14-17,

> And God said, Let there be lights in the firmament of
> the heaven to divide the day from the night; . . .
> And let them be for lights in the firmament of the
> heaven to give light upon the earth: and it was so.
> And God made two great lights; the greater light to
> rule the day, and the lesser light to rule the night: he
> made the stars also.
> And God set them in the firmament of the heaven to
> give light upon the earth.

This day speaks of light-bearing or testimony. But it follows
only after the third day of fruit-bearing. Daniel tells us: "They
that be wise shall shine as the brightness of the firmament; and
they that turn many to righteousness as the stars for ever and
ever" (Daniel 12:3).

Believers should be stars. They are expected to shine. When
Jesus comes to reign on the earth He will come as the *Sun of
Righteousness*. He will flood the earth with His glory. But He,
the Sun, is gone now into Heaven and it is night here on the
earth below. But there is a source of light. We have the moon
and the stars during the night of His rejection and absence. His
Church is here as the moon reflecting the light of the Sun of
Righteousness, and then we are the individual stars to shed forth
His light.

## STANDING AND STATE

Notice, too, the perfect description of the believer's position
in Christ and his walk on earth as given in this fourth day. The
stars are said to be *"set in heaven to give light on the earth."*
Set in heaven! That is where every believer is *in Christ*. God
sees us who have believed *in Christ* as though we were already
seated in Heaven. Paul says that God: ". . . hath quickened us
together with Christ, (by grace ye are saved;) And hath raised
us up together, and made us *sit together in heavenly places in
Christ Jesus*" (Ephesians 2:5, 6).

In Ephesians 5 Paul says that we are "members of his
(Christ's) body, of his flesh, and of his bones" (Ephesians 5:30).
Since our head (Christ) is bodily in Heaven today, we as members of that body are looked upon as already being in Heaven
right now. God looks upon the mystical Body of Christ, the

Church, as already seated in the heavenlies. Paul says of us that God,

> Who is rich in mercy, for his great love wherewith he loved us,
> Even when we were dead in sins, hath quickened us together with Christ, (by grace ye are saved;)
> And hath raised us up together, and made us *sit together in heavenly places in Christ Jesus* (Ephesians 2:4-6).

This is our present position in Christ as God looks upon the believer. We are therefore placed in the heavens like the stars in the sky. We are God's stars, way up there in the heavens.

## SHINE ON EARTH

But while stars are placed in the heavens, they were made to *shine on earth*. The language of Genesis 1:15 is clear that they are lights in the firmament of heaven, *to give light upon the earth*. We are compared to stars. Daniel says: "And they that be wise shall shine as the brightness of the firmament; and they that turn many to righteousness as the stars for ever and ever" (Daniel 12:3).

Christians are stars, set in Heaven, but shining on earth. In Christ we are already in Heaven; in walk and experience we are still on this earth. We are left here to shine among men. This old world lies in darkness. It is groping about seeking a way out and knows not that the only hope is in Christ, and we are expected to tell them about it. When Jesus was here on earth He said, "As long as I am in the world, I am the light of the world" (John 9:5). But that light has gone to Heaven, and men cannot see Him any more. But before He left He committed the light to others who would be here and could be seen by men. He said:

> Ye are the light of the world. A city that is set on an hill cannot be hid . . .
> Let your light so shine *before men*, that they may see your good works, and glorify your Father which is in heaven (Matthew 5:14, 16).

What a solemn commission is ours. The world truly is lost in the darkness of sin. It has no light. But Jesus has made us to be lights in this dark night while the Sun of Righteousness is in Heaven, and has commanded us to *shine*. What are you doing to make Christ known to this poor, Hell-bound generation of today? Oh, there are so many ways you can do it. You can pray, of course. You can give out the message of light in gospel tracts and the Scriptures. You can let your light shine by living a godly life. You can give your testimony and tell men and women about Christ. Maybe you can preach, and if you cannot preach yourself, you can make it possible for others to preach. You can send forth the light by helping those who are broadcasting the Gospel to countless thousands by means of the radio. Oh, do you really appreciate what you have in Christ? that you are seated in Heaven *in Christ* and that you are complete in Him? That very thought ought to make you eager to let your light shine in a hundred different ways.

> Ye are the light of the world. A city that is set on an hill cannot be hid . . .
> Let *your* light so shine before men, that they may see your good works, and glorify your Father which is in heaven (Matthew 5:14, 16).

## Chapter Sixteen

## THE LIFE OF VICTORY

*And God said, Let the waters bring forth abundantly the moving creature that hath life, and fowl that may fly above the earth in the open firmament of heaven.*

*And God created great whales, and every living creature that moveth, which the waters brought forth abundantly, after their kind, and every winged fowl after his kind: and God saw that it was good.*

*And God blessed them, saying, Be fruitful, and multiply, and fill the waters in the seas, and let fowl multiply in the earth.*

*And the evening and the morning were the fifth day (Genesis 1:20-23).*

The story of the physical creation in Genesis 1 is a picture of the Spiritual New Creation. It illustrates the experience of every born-again believer. First God brings out of the chaos of Genesis 1:2, the *light* on the first day. Then He separates the waters in the heavens from those on earth. Then the dry land and plants appear and then follows the setting of the lights in heaven. Every believer is a new creation according to II Corinthians 5:17, "Therefore if any man be in Christ, he is a *new creation.*"

### GROWTH IN GRACE

The Christian life is a growth and development which begins on the day of conversion when God says, "Let there be light." The new-born believer must now learn *separation* from the world first of all. Then he is to become fruitful and reproduce his kind in winning others for Christ. Then he becomes a shining light seated like the stars in the heavens but shining on the earth. All this we have covered. But there is still more. A Christian may be separated from the world and be a soul winner and a testimony and yet lack the absolute victory over the world and sin and self which God has purposed for him. Too many Christians go along defeated and anxious, weak and struggling, up one day and down the next, instead of soaring up into the upper atmosphere of victory in Christ even as a bird defies the pull of earth's gravity and soars into the blue and breathes the pure ozone of the firmament far, far above the din and turmoil of this old earth. God did not save us just to deliver us from Hell and take us to Heaven when we die. Many folks think of salvation as an act of God whereby they are saved from going to Hell and finally go to Heaven when the end comes. But God had a higher aim than that in salvation, and the saving from Hell was merely incidental in this plan.

The goal of the Christian is victory. We are to grow in grace until we rise above every circumstance of life. Like a bird we are to defy the forces which would bind us to earth and rise upon wings of faith into the heavens.

## THE FIFTH DAY OF CREATION

And so on the fifth day of creation we have the life of victory set before us. On that day God made *fish* and *birds*, two of the strangest of God's creatures. A fish has the power to defy the forces of nature. It can sink into the depths of the sea where the water pressure is so great that it would crush any other animal, and then rise to the surface and be just as comfortable, just by adjusting its air-bladder and its cell pressure. It defies the pressure of matter and conquers the death-dealing force of these tons of pressure. But a bird is still more wonderful. It is a creature made up of elements heavier than air. Hence the gravity of the earth holds it down and binds it to this old earth. But a bird can overcome this pull of earth by a very unique method. It can permit another force, an unseen force, to overcome this gravity and lift it up against gravity far up into the heavens. This other force is the air, and all the bird needs to do is to spread its wings and permit the wind (which is air in motion) to get under its pinions and the wind carries the bird up and away from the earth. Now a bird never really flies. Instead it just leans on the wind and lets the wind do the lifting. No bird can fly a foot without wind, any more than you can. Unless there is a wind to get under its wings, it too must be bound to earth. And so on a day when there is no wind, the bird *makes its own wind*. It begins to flap its wings to produce wind; that is, its own wind, and flies away. But it soon tires when there is no wind and presently comes down to earth again. But on a windy day all is different. Now watch that seagull take off. It will just lean into the wind without moving a feather, and soar and soar and soar without any other effort except spreading its wings and letting it bear it away. I have watched eagles that soared for hours in the blue heavens without moving a feather. You have all seen hawks and buzzards do the same thing. The same principle applies to flying. The airplane produces its own wind by rapidly whirling the propeller, resulting in an airfoil which provides the lift; but when there is enough wind a glider can stay aloft for many hours without mechanical power, in fact, as long as there is enough wind.

### THE WIND AND THE FLAPPING

Now the more wind there is, the less flapping is necessary, and the easier it is to rise. The less wind, the more of flapping and effort and work, and the sooner the bird will tire and come to earth again. Now all these things have a lesson for us. In the new creation we find the exact counterpart. God wants us to fly above the din of this old world. He wants us to have victory over the pull of this world and dwell in the place of freedom and liberty, and we accomplish it in the very same way.

### WIND AND SPIRIT

Notice carefully a unique thing in the Scriptures. In the Old Testament Hebrew the very same identical word is used to denote *wind* and *spirit*. The Hebrew word is *ruach*. In some places this word *ruach* is translated *wind* and in other places *spirit*, as the context may indicate. In the New Testament Greek the same is true. The same word is used for "wind" and "spirit" here, too, and the word is *pneuma*. In some places *pneuma* is translated *wind* and in others *spirit*. Spirit means breath, moving air or wind. Let me give an illustration. In John 3 we read: "The wind bloweth where it listeth, and thou hearest the sound thereof, but canst not tell whence it cometh, and whither it goeth: so is every one that is born of the *spirit*" (John 3:8).

Now the same word *pneuma* is translated first *wind* and then at the close of the verse it is rendered *spirit*. But they are the same word and it would be more correct to read the verse thus: "The *Spirit* moveth where He listeth, and ye hear the evidence of Him but know not whence He cometh nor whither He goeth: so is every one that is born of the *Spirit*."

Or take Acts, chapter 2, where we read: "And suddenly there came a sound from heaven as of a rushing mighty wind [*pneuma*], and it filled all the house where they were sitting" (Acts 2:2).

The word translated wind is *pneuma,* the same as the word for *spirit,* and it would be just as correct to read, "there came a sound from heaven as of a rushing mighty *Spirit,* and He filled all the house." It was the Spirit who came and filled the company in the upper room, not *wind.* So the Spirit is to the Christian what the wind is to the bird. It is the Spirit alone who can give us victory over the forces of the old nature which keep pulling us down and holding us to the earth. All we need to do is to extend our wings of faith, yield to that heavenly Wind, and literally lean on that heavenly zephyr, the Holy Spirit, and then *He* lifts us up into the life of victory.

We said that the less wind, the more flapping the bird will have to do, the more wearying and discouraging the process will be, but the more wind, the less flapping and the higher the flight. Yes, thousands of churches and individuals still need to learn this. The more of the Spirit there is in a church, the less need there will be for all the fleshly methods which need to be employed to keep our people happy. The more flesh in our worship, the more flapping. We have to keep our people all pepped up by unscriptural programs to keep them interested. We fill our assemblies with social parlors, pool rooms, moving pictures, church suppers, and cast-off clothing sales, Halloween parties, and father and son banquets. My, what a busy program we have! What a complicated organization. How many boards and committees. Just look at the calendar and see all the doings. See the weekly bulletin and look at the activities. And yet nothing or little is produced in the way of fruit or victory. It is months since a sinner was saved. And many folk think that all this activity is spiritual service. Listen, my friend, the more of the Spirit in the meeting and the church, the less of fleshly flapping there will be. The more the *Spirit* is the organizer of your program, the less of organization you will need. The more the Spirit directs the work of the church the less of the human directors you will need and the more we are led by the Spirit, the fewer the committees and boards and intricate, cut-and-dried programs. The more wind the less flapping, and vice versa. Do not mistake activity for victory.

## TRUE PERSONALLY

And what is true of organizations and groups is true of each individual. The more we yield to the Spirit, the less of fleshly struggle and effort there will be. "This I say then, Walk in the Spirit, and ye shall not fulfil the lust of the flesh" (Galatians 5:16).

Do you have a struggle rising like a bird above the circumstances of life? Then turn it over to Christ and let Him take control. Paul cried out: "O wretched man that I am! who shall deliver me from the body of this death?" (Romans 7:24).

And immediately gave the answer: "I thank God through Jesus Christ our Lord . . ." (Romans 7:25).

Listen again to Paul as he seeks to teach us how to fly: ". . . yield yourselves unto God, as those that are alive from the dead, and your members as instruments of righteousness unto God" (Romans 6:13).

I saw the lesson of yielding to the Spirit illustrated some years ago in a graphic way. We were at a cabin way up in the wilderness of northern Michigan. Each day a huge bald eagle would perch on the top of a dead pine just across the little bay.

He would sit there for some time, eyeing the sun, and then stirred by some strange impulse he would take off. He seemed to wait for just the right wind, and then he would spread his great wings and just lean upon the wind without flapping or moving a feather and spiral up and up. There was no effort — the wind bore him up as he simply leaned upon it, as he rose in even, heightening spirals into the pure ether of the azure blue. Smaller and smaller he became until at last only a speck was left, and then strain my eyes as I would, he was swallowed up in the heavens. No effort, no flapping, just resting as he ascended up and up and up to be lost in the cloudless heavens above, far above the screaming of the clumsy loons and the chatter of the earth-bound chipmunks. And right there I found something. I said, "Oh God, in Jesus' Name, I am weary of the struggle. I too want to be able to soar above it all. I want to dwell where the petty things of life and the fretful flapping of men trouble me no more." And the words came like the soft peal of an evening bell: "Commit thy way unto the Lord; trust also in him; and he shall bring it to pass. Rest in the Lord, and wait patiently for him; fret not thyself . . ." (Psalm 37:5, 7).

And then:

> Be careful for nothing; but in every thing by prayer and supplication with thanksgiving let your requests be made known unto God.
>
> And the *peace of God,* which passeth all understanding, shall keep your hearts and minds through Christ Jesus (Philippians 4:6, 7).

Oh, Christian, there is victory for you if you will turn yourself completely over to Him, even as the eagle rests upon the wind and permits *it* to do the lifting. Do you want that victory? Then just where you are, tell Him about it. Say to Him, "I denounce all my own efforts and confess that by myself I am unable to conquer this thing that holds me down and I am turning it all over to Thee, and trusting, leaning on Thee, resting on the Spirit's power."

As it was the Spirit that brooded upon the soul at conversion, so it is the Spirit who must continue the work until victory is achieved.

*Chapter Seventeen*

# THE IMAGE OF GOD

The Bible describes two acts of creation by God, a material creation and a spiritual creation. The material creation is introduced in the first book of the Bible as follows: "In the beginning God created the heaven and the earth" (Genesis 1:1).

The spiritual creation is described by Paul as follows: "Therefore if any man be in Christ, he is a *new creation*: old things are passed away; behold, all things are become new" (II Corinthians 5:17).

The first creation was a picture of the new creation. The parallel is perfect in its every detail. There are a number of important things about these creations. Notice first that when God creates He begins with *nothing* but Himself. Before God created there was nothing but God — God alone, supreme, sovereign and absolute. This is God's answer to evolution which must of necessity begin with *something*, a nebular mass, a primal cell or a blob of protoplasm. But God begins with *nothing*. The word translated "create" is *bara* in the original. It means to bring into being without any pre-existing material. To emphasize the fact that creation begins with nothing but God — the same word *bara* is used for the *creator* and "to create."

## IN THE SPIRITUAL

The same is true of the new creation. In it God will not use any pre-existent material. He begins from "scratch," he begins with nothing. He will not accept help from anyone else. Before the sinner can become a new creation, he must be reduced to *nothing*. He must abandon his claim to any merit or goodness. He must come with *nothing* — absolutely *nothing*. Salvation is of the Lord. It is all of grace.

119

> Not by works of righteousness which we have done, but according to his mercy he saved us, by the washing of *regeneration,* and renewing of the Holy Ghost (Titus 3:5).
>
> But to him that worketh not, but believeth on him that justifieth the ungodly, his faith is counted for righteousness (Romans 4:5).

God will never be indebted to His creature. The new creation, therefore, is entirely God's work. It is brand new. The new birth is not a re-birth but a "new" birth — a new creation. It is not the old man made over, dressed up, improved or repaired, but a new nature placed within the believer and wholly separate from the old Adamic nature. God begins with nothing but Himself!

## ALL BY THE WORD

The second thing about God's creation — both old and new — is that it is by the *Word of God.* David says: "By the word of the LORD were the heavens made . . ." (Psalm 33:6).

The writer of Hebrews tells us: "Through faith we understand that the worlds were framed by the word of God" (Hebrews 11:3).

And the Apostle Peter adds his testimony to this, and declares: ". . . by the word of God the heavens were of old, and the earth standing out of the water and in the water" (II Peter 3:5).

And what is true of the material creation of Genesis 1:1 is true of the new creation of the born-again believer. No one is ever saved except through the *Word* of God. The Apostle Peter in his first epistle clinches it once and forever: "Being born again, not of curruptible seed, but of incorruptible, by the *Word of God,* which liveth and abideth forever" (I Peter 1:23).

Jesus Christ is the *Word of God,* and since the worlds were created by the Word of God, the Lord Jesus is the Creator. This the Bible also asserts:

> In the beginning was the Word, and the Word was with God, and the Word was God.
>
> The same was in the beginning with God.
>
> All things were made by him; and without him was not any thing made that was made (John 1:1-3).

But the Word of God is also applied to the written Word —
the Scriptures. The Bible is the written record of the Word incarnate. And just as the material creation was by the *Word,*
so the new creation is by this *Word.* Jesus Himself said: "Verily,
verily, I say unto you, He that heareth *my word,* and believeth
on him that sent me, hath everlasting life" (John 5:24).

## GOD SPEAKS

After the Spirit of the Lord brooded over the creation
(Genesis 1:2) God spoke as follows: "And God said, Let there
be light: and there was light" (Genesis 1:3).

God spoke the Word and the light came. So, too, in the new
creation, the "light" broke through when the sinner heard the
Word of God. And all the rest which follows is by the Word.
No less than ten times, exactly ten times, the expression, "And
God said," occurs in the first chapter of Genesis. It began when
God said, "Let there be light." And by that word of God every-
thing which follows came. On the second day, we saw *separation*
by the Word. On the third day there was *fruit* by the Word
of God. On the fourth day there was *testimony* by the Word of
God, and on the fifth day there was *victory* by the Word of God.
We come now to the sixth day of creation and again it is by the
Word of God.

## NO PROGRESS WITHOUT WORD

We must emphasize, therefore, the importance of the Word
of God in the whole plan of salvation. Not only is there no conversion apart from the *Word,* but there can be no progress, no
growth without it. Your growth in grace, in separation, in holiness, in victory, is in direct proportion to your knowledge of
the Word of God. You may sing and testify and pray and work,
and yet get nowhere if you neglect the study of the Word. You
simply cannot know God's will unless you know God's Word.
The greatest tragedy in the average Christian's life is the sad,
sad ignorance of the Book. The reason so many are spiritually
weak, sickly, ennervated, emaciated, anemic, powerless and
faint is because of lack of feeding on the Word of God. If I
were to inquire into your spiritual progress and were permitted

to ask only one question, I would ask, "How much time do you spend with the Word?" I would not ask how faithful you are in going to church, or how loud you testify, or even how much you pray. My first and most important question would be, "How well do you know the Word?" Here lies the greatest weakness of the average believer. May I suggest you take a few minutes to take an inventory of your Bible study habits — if you dare to face it. Here is the answer to personal spiritual development and the key to a revival so much needed. Before leaving this angle of the subject of the new creation, we would refer you to a verse by Peter: "But grow in grace, and in the knowledge of our Lord and Saviour Jesus Christ" (II Peter 3:18).

Notice one word in this verse which is the secret of spiritual growth. It is the word *knowledge*. Our growth in grace is proportionate to our knowledge of Him, and the only way we can know Him is by the Word of God. That is why Paul's great passion was "that I may *know* him" (Philippians 3:10).

## THE FINAL GOAL

We return now to the record of the two creations. We have traced the record in Genesis through the fifth day. The first day was light, a picture of conversion. The second was the day of separation; the third was the day of fruit-bearing; the fourth was testimony, and the fifth speaks of victory as seen in the creation of the birds and fish defying the forces of gravity. One more day of progress remains before we come to the day of completion and rest. On the sixth day God crowns His creation with a creature in the very image of God. On this day God created the land animals, cattle and creeping things and the beasts of the field. And then last of all, God crowns it all with the appearance of *man* — the very image of God.

> And God said, Let us make man in our image, after our likeness: and let them have dominion over the fish of the sea, and over the fowl of the air, and over cattle, and over all the earth, and over every creeping thing that creepeth upon the earth.
> So God created man in his own image, in the image of God created he him; male and female created he them (Genesis 1:26, 27).

The progress of the days of creation, beginning with "Let there be light," climaxes in the image of God. That was the goal of the old creation, the last thing before God rested. That, too, is the goal of the new creation, God's purpose for which He saves every believer. It is not only to save us from Hell, but God's goal, aim, and purpose is to make us ultimately in His very image. And that image of God is Jesus Christ. This is stated clearly in Hebrews:

> Who being the brightness of his glory, and the express *image* of his person, and upholding all things by the word of his power, when he had by himself purged our sins, sat down on the right hand of the Majesty on high (Hebrews 1:3).

Jesus Christ is the express image of God, and God's final purpose for every believer is to make him ultimately *like Jesus,* in the image of God. When God first spoke the word on the first day, "Let there be light," He had in mind the crowning act of creation — the making of a man in the image of God.

Even so when God chose the believer to be saved, He had in mind the consummation of salvation — the perfect image of God, to make us like His Son Jesus Christ. Everything moves toward that goal, expressed in that majestic, inexhaustible, unfathomable passage in Romans 8:28, 29,

> And we know that all things work together for good to them that love God, to them who are the called according to his purpose.
> For whom he did foreknow, he also did predestinate to be conformed to the image of his Son, that he [the Son] might be the firstborn among many brethren (Romans 8:28, 29).

God's final purpose for which the believer is predestinated is to become ultimately like Jesus Christ. Someone has said, "God was so pleased with His Son Jesus Christ that He wanted a whole heaven full of others just like Him, and so He predestinated a great company of 'many brethren' with Jesus as the firstborn." To accomplish this we read in Romans 8:30, "Moreover whom he did predestinate, them he also called: and whom he called, them he also justified: and whom he justified, them he also glorified."

And so God completed His work of six days' creation by making man in His image, and then He rested on the seventh day. God did not rest until He had made man in His own image. And beloved, God will not rest until you and I as believers have reached that place of conformity to the image of His Son which will fit us for our eternal abode with Him. As we come to the close of our discussion of God's work in the new creation, may we ask, "How far have you gone toward this goal?" If you are saved, have you gone the second step — separation from sin and evil? Then have you reached the third day of fruit-bearing and soul winning? How about your testimony on day number four? And your victory on the fifth day? Soon you shall come to the end of the road, and what is incomplete then will have to be completed at the Judgment Seat of Christ, for God will fulfill His purpose of reproducing the image of Christ in you. Why not conform to His will now, and not have to see all your works go up in smoke at the Judgment Seat, and finally be "saved so as by fire," and "suffer loss," and "be ashamed at his coming," and "lose your reward."

> For we must all appear before the judgment seat of Christ; that every one may receive the things done in his body, according to that he hath done, whether it be good or bad (II Corinthians 5:10).

## Chapter Eighteen

## THREE STEPS TO MODERNISM

*Now the serpent was more subtil than any beast of the field which the Lord God had made. And he said unto the woman, Yea, hath God said, Ye shall not eat of every tree of the garden? (Genesis 3:1).*

This is the first verse in the Bible with a question mark after it. All the preceding statements in the first two chapters of Genesis are declarations of truth which only the Devil and his followers doubt. But when we come to this first verse in Genesis 3, the great heart chapter of Genesis, we meet with a question, and we are not surprised, when we realize who it is that is speaking. It is none other than the serpent — Satan incarnated in the most beautiful beast of the field which God had made. And it is the Devil who asks the first question in the Bible, casts the first doubt upon the Word of the Lord, and by clever deception gains the ear of Mother Eve. Satan is the great deceiver. He comes in the garb of a beautiful animal, walking upright in all its dignity and with the power of speech, the only instance in nature of a beast being able to communicate with man, except by special permission of God. The word *serpent* means the "whisperer" and this itself is highly suggestive. And this tempter comes to Mother Eve and asks,

### Yea, Hath God Said?

By careful innuendo he plants the seed of doubt in Eve's mind and then misrepresents God. He says, "Yea, hath God said, Ye shall not eat of every tree of the garden?" What a foolish question, and we marvel that Eve gave him an answer at all. If God had forbidden them to eat of *every* tree of the garden, then how in the world were Adam and Eve to live? There was as yet no death, for there was no sin, and hence Adam and Eve were pure vegetarians and could not eat meat. They were therefore limited to a vegetable diet, and yet the Devil dared to ask, casting aspersion on God's goodness, "Did God really forbid you to eat of *any* tree in the garden?"

Now notice carefully the answer of Eve, for in this answer we have the nature and the beginning and character of all sin. Most people think of sin as an act rather than an attitude. It is generally believed that Eve sinned when she actually ate of the tree which God had forbidden, but this is hardly true. Eve's sin was committed before that, when she *believed* the Devil instead of God. That was the root of her sin and the act of taking of the fruit was only the natural result of her unbelief of the Word of the Lord. Sin is not primarily an act but an *attitude* toward God. We think of murder as sin, but the Bible says, "He that hateth his brother is a murderer." We think of immoral acts as sin, but Jesus said, "He that looketh upon a woman to lust after her hath already committed adultery in his heart." Stealing and theft is not the real sin, but the covetousness which results in sin. Sin then is not in the hand that takes the forbidden fruit, but in the heart which does not believe God's Word. This is tersely summed up in the epistle of James when he says:

> But every man is tempted, when he is drawn away of his own lust, and enticed.
> Then when lust hath conceived, it bringeth forth sin: and sin, when it is finished, bringeth forth death (James 1:14, 15).

Just because a man has not been guilty of overt acts of sin and violence does not mean that he is not a sinner. The act is that which man sees; the motive is that which God sees. Man looketh on the outward appearance, but God looketh upon the heart. And Jesus puts it even more clearly when He states:

> Not that which goeth into the mouth defileth a man; but that which cometh out of the mouth, this defileth a man.
> But those things which proceed out of the mouth come forth from the heart; and they defile the man.
> For out of the heart proceed evil thoughts, murders, adulteries, fornication, thefts, false witness, blasphemies:
> These are the things which defile a man (Matthew 15:11, 18-20).

If ever there was a need for preaching this aspect of sin, it is today when men boast of their own goodness and self-righteousness, and just because they live outwardly good and moral lives, deceive themselves into thinking they are not sinners and do not need a Saviour. But once we look at sin as God sees it, as a thing of the heart and as unbelief, we can endorse the indictment of Paul in Romans 3:23, "For all have sinned, and come short of the glory of God."

The Bible taking this view of sin declares that "there is none righteous, no not one." It will do no good to measure ourselves by the standards of men, for after all, we are going to be judged by the standards of God and His Word. In God's sight all are sinners and need the cleansing blood of the Lord Jesus Christ. There is no other way.

### EVE AS AN EXAMPLE

And so the Spirit of God has inserted in the record in Genesis 3, this account of the sin of Eve in the garden. So we repeat, Eve sinned when she doubted God's Word and listened to the Devil. All the rest followed in a most natural way. Notice, therefore, what Eve said to the serpent:

> And the woman said unto the serpent, We may eat of the fruit of the trees of the garden:
> But of the fruit of the tree which is in the midst of the garden, God hath said, Ye shall not eat of it, neither shall ye touch it, *lest* ye die (Genesis 3:2, 3).

Right there Eve fell, right there Eve sinned, and the subsequent eating of the fruit was only the result of this first sin. The first sin of Eve was doubting God, and the next was *lying*. Eve was a liar. Before she became a thief, she was a liar, and before she was a liar she was an unbeliever. Now don't wince at this, for it is right here in the record. What Eve quoted God as saying was an untruth; God never said that at all. Compare the two statements. God had said:

> . . . of every tree of the garden thou mayest freely eat:
> But of the tree of the knowledge of good and evil, thou shalt not eat of it: for in the day thou eatest thereof thou shalt surely die (Genesis 2:16, 17).

Compare that with Eve's statement, "Ye shall not eat of it, *lest ye die!*" God said, "Thou shalt *surely die.*" Eve said, "*Lest ye die."* There is a great difference in those two statements. The first is a *certainty;* the second is a *possibility.* Eve misquoted God's Word, she lied and quoted God as saying something He had never said. God says, *surely;* the devil says *not* surely; Eve says *lest* ye die.

Now in examining this statement of Mother Eve we find that she made three mistakes, which always lead to disaster. First, she added something to God's Word. Second, she changed something in the Word of God, and then, finally, she left something out of the Word of God. Notice each one of these.

First, she added something to the Word, "neither shall ye touch it." Now God had merely prohibited *eating.* He had said nothing about *touching.* That was Eve's own interpretation, and she added it. Second, she changed something in the Word. She changed the certainty to a bare possibility by saying, "Lest ye die," instead of "Thou shalt surely die." And finally, she left out the most important part of God's Word, *surely.* God had said, "Thou shalt surely die." From there on the rest was easy, and the record goes on to say that she looked at the tree, desired it, and ate of it, and fell and found out that in spite of her own interpretation of what God meant, it still was true and she died.

## EVE A VERY MODERN PERSON

In these three steps Eve acted the part of a thoroughly modern, twentieth century unbeliever. Here is where infidelity begins and it always follows the same course. First, men *add* something to God's Word. It makes little difference *what* they add; adding *anything* to God's Word can only lead to the next downward step of infidelity. Here lies the root and beginning of all false doctrines, adding something to the Word. It may be your own interpretation or a religious creed or dogma or statement of belief or an additional revelation; whatever it is, God will not countenance any addition to His Word. The wide and varied differences today among those who call themselves Christian are all based upon certain interpretations of Scripture which are accepted as equal authority with the Word of God. What is Catholicism but the Bible *plus* the traditions of the church, papal bulls, and church doctrines? What is Seventh-day Adventism but the Bible *plus* the prophecies of Mrs. White? What is Mormonism but the Bible *plus* the wholly fictitious golden tablets of a Joseph Smith? What is Christian Science but the Bible *plus* Mary Baker Glover Patterson Eddy's "Key to the Scriptures"?

Right here it would not be amiss to sound a warning to others who, while considered orthodox and sound, still are in the same danger. The moment we give our church creeds and confessions a place of authority equal with or a place approximately equal with the Bible we have taken the first step in the direction to modernism. It makes no difference whether this be the Westminster Confession or the Heidelburg Catechism or the Augsburg Confession or the Auburn Confession or any other. The Bible *alone* must remain the sole and inviolable authority for faith and practice, or we shall soon find ourselves where Eve began.

## THE SECOND STEP

Now the second step immediately follows. When we add our own creeds or dogmas or confessions or statements of faith to the Bible, it usually does not take long until we find that the Bible and our additions do not always harmonize, and because man is too proud as a rule to admit that he is wrong, he will seek in every way possible to twist the Bible in order to make it fit his creed and his interpretations. Hence, texts will be taken out of their setting, Scriptures will be spiritualized, and the Bible twisted and forced to make it endorse and prove our belief and interpretation.

## THE THIRD STEP

Then comes the third step. Sooner or later it is found that there are some Scriptures which cannot even be twisted enough to back up our interpretations, and then there is only one thing left to do, *get rid of those parts of the Bible* which do not fit in with our ideas. Before long most of the Bible is deleted, until there is nothing left but the Ten Commandments which no man keeps, the Sermon on the Mount which no one practices, and the Lord's Prayer which Jesus gave to His disciples, and the Beatitudes. This, beloved, is the beginning, growth, and fruitage of modern-day liberalism, which began way yonder in the Garden of Eden by Mother Eve.

Now go on and see what the result is. The enemy was quick to detect Eve's most vulnerable spot and gives the reply: "And the serpent said unto the woman, Ye shall not surely die" (Genesis 3:4).

Ye shall not surely die! God had said, *surely*. The Devil says *not surely*. And then he becomes bolder and begins to poison the mind of Eve as to the honesty and dependability of God, for he adds immediately: "For God doth know that in the day ye eat thereof, then your eyes shall be opened, and ye shall be as gods, knowing good and evil" (Genesis 3:5).

How clever! The Devil says, and he must have whispered this, "God is keeping something from you. There is something wonderful for you, but God does not want you to have it." And then he adds this tempting morsel, "Ye shall know good and evil." Now that was a blind package for Eve, for she as yet knew nothing about evil, for the knowledge of good and evil could only come through eating of the forbidden tree. And Eve was convinced that God had not been fair and honest with them and was keeping something back, and she believed this superlatively beautiful creature, the serpent, with his smooth words and his soft pleasant voice and his re-assurance that things were not as bad as the Word of God would make them.

And listen, my friend, the tactics of Satan have not changed one bit until this day. Satan's methods worked so well the first time when he tried them on Eve, that he has never had occasion to alter his approach. Since Eve's day he has tried it on countless millions of Eve's hapless descendants with stunning and telling effect. And I want to warn you against it, for it is very subtle. The Word of God says, "The soul that sinneth it shall die." "The wages of sin is death." "The wicked shall be turned into hell, and every nation that forgets God." The Bible says you are a sinner, and unless you repent and believe on the Lord Jesus Christ you are lost forever, and will have to spend eternity in the lake of fire, in outer darkness, separated from God and His love throughout all eternity. God says this is a certainty. And the same old deceiver comes and says, "Don't you believe it; it is not as bad as all that. God will not punish His creature in an eternal Hell. 'Thou shalt not surely die.' Don't be alarmed. You are not as bad as the Bible says." Listen, my friend, it is the Devil's same old lie which he told in the Garden of Eden and the result will be the same. It is God's Word against the Devil's and common sense alone should tell you who is right, for the Devil is a liar from the beginning.

In the next chapter, we shall take up the result in detail and see how Eve found out what a big liar the Devil is, but when she found out, it was too late. But in concluding this chapter, I want to plead with each of you who read this message not to make the mistake which Eve made. It is merely a question of *whom will you believe?* Jesus said:

> He that believeth on him is not condemned: but he that believeth not is condemned already, because he hath not believed in the name of the only begotten Son of God (John 3:18).

Whom will you believe? Some time ago I was dealing with a man and he said to me, "I don't believe what you say at all, or what the Bible says. You say that if I reject Jesus Christ, I will perish forever in a Bible hell. Well, go ahead and believe it, and go your way, I simply don't see it that way, and my idea is as good as yours." Well, my answer was, "Wait a minute, friend, that does not settle it; neither what you say nor what I say. The odds are all in my favor. Suppose *you are right*, and there is no life after death, no future Heaven to gain, no Hell to endure. Suppose you are right. I am not losing a thing. I am happy in what I believe, and if at the end I wake up and find I was wrong, I have lost nothing. I have enjoyed my faith — you were right, and this is the end. I have lost nothing. But listen, my friend, *suppose you are wrong* and I am right, then you have lost everything, and may God have mercy upon you. I have nothing to lose if you are right, and everything to gain if you are wrong. But *you, you,* you have everything to lose and nothing to gain." Think it over, my friend; think it over. God says that He —

> . . . will render to every man according to his deeds: To them who by patient continuance in well doing seek for glory and honour and immortality, *eternal life*:
>
> But unto them that . . . do not obey the truth . . . indignation and wrath,
>
> Tribulation and anguish, upon every soul of man that doeth evil (Romans 2:6-9).

Which will you believe? This Word of God — or the Devil?

## Chapter Nineteen

## FIG LEAVES

*And when the woman saw that the tree was good for food, and that it was pleasant to the eyes, and a tree to be desired to make one wise, she took of the fruit thereof, and did eat, and gave also unto her husband with her; and he did eat.*

*And the eyes of them both were opened, and they knew that they were naked; and they sewed fig leaves together, and made themselves aprons (Genesis 3:6, 7).*

In the preceding chapter, we saw that Eve fell, not when she reached forth her hand to take of the forbidden tree, but she fell when she *doubted* the Word of God and gave ear to the tempter Satan, speaking to her through the serpent in the Garden of Eden. In the passage before us now we have the threefold temptation which followed the threefold mistake Eve made when she: (1) *added* to the Word of God; (2) *changed* the Word of God; and (3) *took something away* from the Word of God. In verses 6 and 7 of Genesis 3 we also have three definite things. Eve *saw* the fruit of the tree, that it was good for *food*, good for *sight*, and good for *wisdom*. Three things, *food, sight, wisdom!* The appeal of the temptation attacked Eve in three spheres of her being: *body, soul* and *spirit*.

When God created man He created him in His own image. This image meant first of all that man in creation was patterned after the being of God, *in God's likeness*. Now God is a Trinity in unity. He is one God, but revealed in the Bible as being *three persons* in one God. The Bible from cover to cover thus presents God as being Father, Son, and Holy Spirit. Now when God made man, He followed this pattern and man as he came from the hand of God was also a trinity in unity, *one personality*, but consisting of a *body,* a *soul,* and a *spirit.* This is clearly stated: "And the Lord God formed man of the dust of the ground [*body*], and breathed into his nostrils the breath of life [*spirit*]; and man became a living *soul*" (Genesis 2:7).

When man fell this image was lost, for man died spiritually and ultimately physically as well. Now each one of these parts of the human trinity has its own peculiar characteristics and functions. The body is the seat of the appetite, the soul is the seat of the emotions and worship, while the spirit is the part which is able to know God, the seat of spiritual wisdom in apprehending his Creator, a faculty which no animal has, because the animals are body and soul, and devoid of spirit with which to know and appreciate its Creator.

## The Trinity was Tempted

When the temptation came through Satan to Eve, she was tempted in all three parts of her being, *body, soul,* and *spirit.* All three are separately mentioned in the text. First the temptation of her body came through the channel of the appetite; she saw that the tree was good for *food.* The first temptation, therefore, was to the *physical* side of Eve, her desire for food. The second temptation was to the soul. She saw that it was *pleasant to the eyes.* The soul is the seat of appreciation of beauty, the seat of our appreciation of our likes and dislikes, our ability to enjoy pleasure, and the seat of the emotions. The most common channel to the soul is the eye; therefore, while most temptations of the flesh come through the body, the temptation to the soul comes through the eye. Someone has aptly said, "The eye is the window of the soul." The third temptation came to the spirit of man. Eve saw that it was a tree desired to make one *wise,* undoubtedly the wisdom which the serpent had promised her when he said, "Ye shall be as gods, *knowing* good and evil."

In these three temptations we have summed up every temptation man is subject to. Every temptation of life falls under one of these three: *body, soul,* and *spirit; food, pleasure,* and *knowledge.* There are no other temptations known to man. They correspond to the flesh, the world, and the Devil. John tells us in his first epistle that this is all the temptation there is in this old wicked world: "For all that is in the world, the lust of the flesh, and the lust of the eyes, and the pride of life, is not of the Father, but is of the world" (I John 2:16).

There they are: food, pleasure, and knowledge called here "the pride of life." Everything in the way of temptation is summed up in these three, and when Satan tempted Eve she fell in all three departments and, therefore, her fall was complete. Man is not sick through sin; he is dead. His whole being came under the curse of sin. And it is a significant fact that when Jesus was led into the wilderness to be tempted of the Devil, He met these same three temptations. Jesus went into the wilderness to be tempted as the *second Adam,* to prove first of all that Adam did not have to sin. It was possible for Adam to have resisted, and Jesus proved this by going as the Second Adam, as a man, to meet the same temptation as the first Adam, and yet did not yield nor fall. And Jesus met the tempter under even greater odds than our first father. Adam was tempted in a garden; Jesus in a wilderness. Adam was among the tame beasts of the garden; Jesus was among the wild beasts of the desert, Mark tells us. Adam was not weakened by starvation when he was tempted, but Jesus was hungry after forty days of fasting. And yet Jesus met that same tempter and the very same temptations.

### FIRST TO THE BODY

The first temptation Jesus experienced was the one Eve met first, the appeal to the appetite. The Devil said to the hungering Jesus: ". . . If thou be the Son of God, command this stone that it be made bread" (Luke 4:3).

The appeal is through the eye, and the Devil shows Him food, which John calls the lust of the flesh. The appeal was to the body. Then followed the second temptation through the eyes of Jesus:

> And the devil, taking him up into an high mountain, shewed unto him all the kingdoms of the world in a moment of time.
> And the devil said unto him, . . .
> If thou therefore wilt worship me, all shall be thine (Luke 4:5-7).

The appeal is through the eye and the Devil shows Him the glories of the kingdoms of the world, but again Jesus resists this temptation of the lust of the eyes. And then comes the spiritual temptation, or as John calls it, "The pride of life."

> And he brought him to Jerusalem, and set him on a pinnacle of the temple, and said unto him, If thou be the Son of God, cast thyself down from hence:
> For it is written, He shall give his angels charge over thee, to keep thee (Luke 4:9, 10).

Here is the appeal to wisdom, the appeal of the tree desired to make one wise. As though Satan said, Find out for yourself whether this word is true. Try it out, cast yourself down. But in every case the tempter failed utterly. I believe with all my heart that the victory which the Lord Jesus gained over the tempter could have been Adam and Eve's as well. For instead of doubting God's Word, Jesus quoted God's Word. In each case Jesus answers, "It is written." Four things gained the victory for Jesus. Luke tells us that when Jesus went to the wilderness, He was *full of the Holy Ghost*. And this fullness had resulted from His obedience in the waters of baptism. We are told that Jesus was baptized to fulfill all righteousness. He was obedient to His mission. Further we are told that as He was being baptized, Jesus was *praying* (Luke 3:21). Notice the four things which Jesus did:

1. He was obedient.
2. He was praying.
3. He was filled with the Spirit.
4. He met every temptation with the Word of God.

Surely if our first parents had done the same, they would not have fallen, and in an even more practical vein, it is true that if you and I meet every temptation in this same fourfold way, we need never fall.

### BACK TO EVE AGAIN

But now back to the story in Genesis 3 again. See the awful result of the disobedience of Eve. It is well to repeat again with emphasis that seventh verse which seems to sum up in terrifying brevity the story of human depravity as the result of sin: "And the eyes of them both were opened, and they knew that they were naked; and they sewed fig leaves together, and made themselves aprons" (Genesis 3:7).

Their eyes were opened to sin and closed to holiness. They learned something they had never known before: they were naked before God. They forgot something they had known before: that God was their friend, but their eyes were blinded to that; and so they flee from God and hide in the garden and seek to cover their own nakedness and sin by the work of their own hands. Before they sinned, they had been clothed by a garment of sinlessness and perfection and holiness and now suddenly they find they are without it and are naked. Behold the awful effect of sin! Man knows he has sinned, but he does not know the remedy. His entire concept of God is changed and twisted and distorted. He misunderstands God and His love. He thinks now that God is someone to fear rather than One who has the only remedy for his condition. He hides from God, he makes excuses, he lies, and, foolish, foolish sinner, he imagines he can do something himself to make amends for his wrong. He imagines that by the work of his hands he can recover the garment of holiness and make himself again presentable before God.

*They sewed fig leaves together and made themselves aprons.* Sin does not need a covering; it needs an atonement. The mistake which Adam made is the mistake of all ages, thinking that sin is something on the outside which can be covered by our own works and our own efforts. But sin is in the heart; fig leaves can only cover the external shame of sin, but it can never take it away; it cannot remove the penalty of death. They sewed fig leaves together and made themselves aprons.

## Fig Leaves

We have before mentioned the rule of Bible interpretation we call "the rule of first mention." We repeat it here. It is this: "The first time a word, phrase or incident occurs in the Bible, it gives the meaning to its use anywhere else in the Bible."

What fig leaves mean here, they will mean anywhere else they are mentioned. Jesus in speaking to the Nation of Israel likens them to a fig tree having nothing but leaves, meaning that they depended upon their own righteousness and good works for salvation, rather than the righteousness which only God can provide. Paul says in Romans: "For they being ignorant of God's righteousness, and going about to establish their own righteousness, have not submitted themselves unto the righteousness of God" (Romans 10:3).

*Fig leaves all over again!* Fig leaves then, in the Scriptures, represent man's own efforts to save himself and make himself right with God once more. Adam started the fad of fig-leaf dresses, and every Adam's son born from that day until now has tried the same thing until convicted by the Spirit of God of the necessity of God's remedy and God's righteousness for salvation. Every effort of man without the blood of Christ is an abomination in the sight of God. Fig leaves! Religion cannot save a man. It is only fig leaves. Morality, desirable as it is, and much as all men should be moral, cannot save a man — this, too, is fig leaves. Good works, acts of charity, reformation, education, legislation, can never substitute for God's regeneration. They are fig leaves. God was soon to teach Adam this lesson when He provided a substitutionary sacrifice in Genesis 3:21. We shall take up that matter in a coming message.

There is only one remedy for sin, God's remedy of the blood. Everything else is fig leaves. I hear one say, I do the best I know how. Fig leaves, my friend, fig leaves. Adam did his best, too, but it was not enough. Well, but you say, I go to church and say my prayers and read my Bible every day. That's fine, but without a personal acceptance of Jesus Christ as your Saviour, all that too is fig leaves, nice ones, I will admit, but fig leaves. Another says, I try to live a good, clean, moral, law-abiding life, and I think if I do that I am as good as anyone else and stand as much chance of going to Heaven as anyone else. That too is fine. You ought to live a good, moral law-abiding life. Everyone ought to do that, and if you don't you will soon find yourself in jail. That is the least any man should do, but as far as earning your salvation is concerned, all this is just a nicely, prettily embroidered apron of fig leaves, and God looks right straight through it. God says, "By the works of the law shall no flesh be justified in My sight." God says, "not by works of righteousness which we have done, but according to his mercy he saved us, by the washing of regeneration." Jesus said to one of the finest, moral, upright, religious, law-abiding, respectable men of His day, "Ye *must* be born again." Stop hiding behind your flimsy fig leaves and let God clothe you with the garments of salvation through the blood of Christ.

> . . . Believe on the Lord Jesus Christ, and thou shalt be saved . . . (Acts 16:31).

## Chapter Twenty

## THE UNIVERSAL CONSCIOUSNESS

*And when the woman saw that the tree was good for food, and that it was pleasant to the eyes, and a tree to be desired to make one wise, she took of the fruit thereof, and did eat; and gave also unto her husband with her; and he did eat.*

*And the eyes of them both were opened, and they knew that they were naked; and they sewed fig leaves together, and made themselves aprons (Genesis 3:6, 7).*

Dressmaking is an ancient vocation, dating back to the dawn of human history. In fact, it was the first occupation which man ever chose for himself. God had commanded Adam to be a gardener and to dress the Garden of Eden, but when sin entered, man chose to become a dressmaker and to dress himself. The second occupation was that of farming, which was taken up by Cain, and the third occupation was that of shepherding as seen in the record of Abel. And these three have remained the primary concern of the human race ever since. The matter of keeping the body warm and clothed, and the matter of providing food for the body are the barest essentials of all human need. While Adam did not primarily become a dressmaker to keep warm, it is still true that clothes should be worn for warmth as well as for modesty.

Practically all of man's endeavors have to do with these things. His problem is how to protect the body from the cold, and so we build houses, produce fuel, and make clothes. The other need is food, and the rest of mankind is occupied in raising food and producing meat for food. Well, it all began way back with the first human family and is just as true today. These are the needs and essentials of physical life. But these first dressmakers were a sorry pair. Imagine two adults created in the image of God, cringing among the shrubbery of the garden and frantically gathering fig leaves and sewing them into flimsy aprons to hide their shame which sin had caused. The record is a picture of the entire human race as a result of sin, for all the offspring of Adam have followed their father's footsteps and vocation, and have been doing the same thing ever since, hiding from God, and seeking by the work of their own hands to produce a covering for sin and shame, and yet failing miserably just like father Adam did. Many are the lessons to be learned from this first human pair making their first dresses, and we shall have time to mention only the most important ones.

## MAN KNOWS HE IS NAKED

The first lesson we learn is that sin gave man a conscience of good and evil. Before the fall, man had not known wrong or sin, but when he fell, his eyes were opened and a consciousness of guilt he had never known before crept over him. And this consciousness of guilt is the heritage of the entire human race. The tree in the garden was called the tree of the knowledge of good and evil, and may therefore be called the tree of *conscience*. Paul tells us in Romans that this conscience is the portion of all men everywhere and in every age, even among those who have never had the Gospel or heard the message of sin and salvation. From ice-capped pole to ice-capped pole and around the equator, wherever man is found, there is this knowledge and an effort on the part of men to make amends for and cover his sin before the gods. In heathen lands this consciousness is universal. A tribe or people has never been found who do not have some sort of religion and some sort of ritual for the appeasement of the gods. It is just the repetition of Adam and his fig leaves.

But this knowledge is not confined to the savages and pagans, but is found as well in the most enlightened, cultured and civilized people of the earth as well. It may not take the form of worshiping literal idols or indulging in gory pagan orgies of sacrifice, but the principle is the same. Man knows there is something wrong and is determined to do something about it, but without the Word of God and the light of the Holy Spirit it can only result in failure and a repetition of fig-leaf aprons. The hundreds of agencies all over the world and in every community for the suppression of crime, the lessening of juvenile delinquency, the education of the masses, the religious efforts to improve men morally and ethically and spiritually are all evidences of the fact that man knows there is something radically wrong, and efforts must be made to correct these matters. Now we have no objection to any movement or agency or organization which seeks to stop crime and immorality and drunkenness. We heartily endorse every sincere effort to do something about the matter of juvenile delinquency and the grievous divorce problem. However, we must recognize that the Bible has the only remedy, and that God's way of dealing with these matters is the only permanent way which goes to the root of the problem; namely, the heart of man. All these other efforts must ultimately fail and be only fig leaves of human effort which may result in suppressing and covering up the effects of sin, but can never change the heart of man.

What is needed is a change of *heart* by the blood of God's own substitute. Without this, all human agencies and efforts can at best only control and inhibit sin, but cannot take away the desire and tendency to sin. All men are sinners and need to become new creatures before there can be any permanent help. To educate a sinner can only make an educated sinner, but he is still a sinner. To make sinners religious only makes religious sinners, and I have found them to be the worst rascals of all. Culture can only make cultured sinners. You may reform the sinner, but he will only be a reformed sinner. And so, as a result of many human efforts, the world is full of religious, cultured, polished sinners, but God says, *Ye must be born again.* "The heart of man is deceitful above all things, and desperately wicked." And so all these efforts, while they may represent man's sincere and best efforts, are ultimately futile without God's own remedy for sin, a new heart through faith in Jesus Christ.

If you want to help your community most, get people saved. The best way you can help the police department is to get people saved. The best way to meet the problem of immortality is to get people saved. The best way to solve the juvenile delinquency problem is to get youngsters saved. Statistics of the FBI and reports from judges all over the land show that almost all the crimes of juveniles are by youngsters who come from broken homes, and an amazingly small number from those who have attended church and Sunday school. Do you want to help those agencies which are trying to combat the evil of drunkenness? Then get the drunkard saved, and every time you do, the saloon loses a customer; get enough saved and the saloons will go out of business. Ah, my friend, don't you see where the remedy lies? Not just the fig leaves of human efforts and education and resolutions, but a *new heart*. All this the story of Adam teaches us. I suppose Adam was sincere, desperately sincere as he entered the dressmaking business, but he was sincerely wrong, as God revealed later on, and which we shall discuss at length in the next chapter. Oh, if we, as we seek to meet those social and moral problems, would only follow God's Word and instructions, we should be spared the disappointment of seeing crime and sin increasing in spite of the millions that are being spent to curb it.

## No Use to Hide From God

Now back once again to the story in Genesis 3. The results of sin are graphically shown in this simple record. Not only did Adam and Eve become conscious of their sin and nakedness, but sin distorted and twisted their whole conception of the nature of God. They were afraid of the only One who was able to help them. They did everything they could for themselves, but refused to permit the Lord, the only One who could possibly be of any help, to do anything at all for them. And here comes one of the most gracious suggestions in the whole narrative. God saw their plight and He made the first move to help them. Man by nature will never come to God for help. So blind is he that unless God takes the first step and comes to the sinner, he would be eternally lost. And so while Adam was seeking to hide, God was seeking to find the sinner. Salvation is of the Lord. By nature and apart from the Word of God and His Holy Spirit, no sinner would ever come to God or cry to Him for salvation. The moment the first pang of conviction grips the sinner and the moment he cries to God for mercy, it is already the work of the Holy Spirit. For man is dead in trespasses and in sins, and a dead man can neither cry, nor come, nor believe. All of it is the result of God's seeking the sinner and quickening him by His Holy Spirit. Think of it, over nineteen hundred years before you were born, God already sent His Son into the world that you might be saved *today*. You certainly had nothing to do with that. Way back there in the counsel of eternity, He already planned salvation for fallen humanity as yet uncreated, and in the fullness of time He sent His Son to save *you*. Yes, God first sought the sinner and He seeks you today. The very fact you are hearing this message is God's seeking you now.

## God Seeks the Sinner

Listen to the record once more as given in this wonderful chapter in Genesis 3:

> And they heard the voice of the Lord God walking in the garden in the cool of the day: and Adam and his wife hid themselves from the presence of the Lord God amongst the trees of the garden.
> And the Lord God called unto Adam, and said unto him, Where art thou?
> And he said, I heard thy voice in the garden, and I was afraid, because I was naked; and I hid myself (Genesis 3:8-10).

And then Adam begins to make excuses. God says, "Who told thee that thou wast naked?" And Adam blamed his wife, and the wife blamed the serpent, but all to no avail. Excuses could not do any good. What they needed was God's remedy. Away with fig leaves and find shelter under the blood of the Lamb which God slew for them as we read in Genesis 3:21, "Unto Adam also and to his wife did the Lord God make coats of skins, and clothed them."

Oh, my friend, why don't you let God save you now? You too have heard His voice in the garden saying, Sinner, where art thou? Come out of hiding. Let Me save you. Or have you like Adam hidden behind the flimsy fig-leaf aprons of your own pet excuses? I hear one of you saying, "I don't understand the Bible." Well, bless your heart, you don't need to understand it. God only asks that you believe His promise and offer of salvation. The plea for understanding is just fig leaves, my friend, fig leaves. Another says, "Yes, I would like to be saved, but I don't feel it." More fig leaves, friend. God does not ask you to feel but repent and believe. You certainly don't want to depend on your feelings. I know *I* don't, for my feelings change day by day, and sometimes many times a day. Sometimes I feel good, and then not so good. My feelings depend on circumstances and conditions, and on my digestion and condition of my liver, and a hundred other things. My feelings change constantly, but *God's promises* never change. Don't trust your feelings, but trust *Him* and His Word. When you really receive the Lord Jesus, you will get plenty of feelings, and good ones, too, but don't wait for feelings before you are saved. They are just fig leaves!

Still another says, "I am not so bad. I do my best and I'll take my chance on that." Well, your best is fig leaves, too, for your best is not good enough for God. He says, "There is *none* righteous, there is none that doeth good." "No," says another, "that is not my trouble. I am not good enough. I am altogether too bad and too wicked." Fig leaves all over again. You don't wait until you feel better before you go to the doctor, do you? Of course, you are not good enough. If you were, you would not need a Saviour. Jesus said, "I am come not to call the righteous, but sinners to repentance." The very fact that you are *not* good enough is the best reason in the world to come to Jesus, and the worse you are, the more you need Him.

Well, says still another, the reason I am not a Christian is because there are too many hypocrites in the church. Fig leaves, friend. Better get rid of them. Who said anything about joining church? I am asking you to *join* the Body of Christ, the One True Church and be saved. Then you join any church the Lord leads you to, if you can find one without hypocrites where all the people are as good as you are. That excuse is by far the flimsiest, most transparent fig-leaf apron anyone could weave. Just remember, if you reject Christ, you will go to the same place where all the hypocrites go, and if you hate them so much, you had better avoid that place and come to Christ.

We might go on and on with dozens of other excuses which

men raise, but like all the rest, they are only *fig leaves*. Why not face the issue squarely and admit that you need a Saviour, and believe God's Word, and be saved? Cast away all your cobweb garments of excuses and accept God's estimate of yourself, and then take His remedy, repentance toward God and faith in Jesus Christ. There is a verse in Isaiah 59 with which I shall close. The chapter begins with these words:

> Behold, the LORD's hand is not shortened, that it cannot save; neither his ear heavy, that it cannot hear:
> But your iniquities have separated between you and your God, and your sins have hid his face from you, that he will not hear (Isaiah 59:1, 2).

Israel had tried to cover their sins by outward works of righteousness and religious observances and good works, but God says these will not cover sin and then adds in verse 6:

> Their webs shall not become garments, neither shall they cover themselves with their works: their works are works of iniquity, and the act of violence is in their hands (Isaiah 59:6).

Their webs shall not become garments! Oh, flee to Christ today, forsake your fig-leaf aprons, cast away all your excuses, believe on the Lord Jesus Christ, and thou shalt be saved (Acts 16:31).

## Chapter Twenty-one

## ONLY TWO RELIGIONS

*And the eyes of them both were opened, and they knew that they were naked; and they sewed fig leaves together, and made themselves aprons (Genesis 3:7).*

*Unto Adam also and to his wife did the Lord God make coats of skins, and clothed them (Genesis 3:21).*

*. . . and the blood of Jesus Christ his Son cleanseth us from all sin (I John 1:7).*

Fig leaves in the Bible represent man's own futile and useless effort to save himself. Blood, on the other hand, speaks of God's only plan of salvation. These two represent the only two religions the world has ever known. While we classify for convenience many hundreds of religions, there are in reality only two: *Man's* efforts, and *God's* salvation. We meet these in the very dawn of human history and the two are placed together in the third chapter of Genesis so that man may never forget the lesson. No sooner had man broken with his God and sinned, than he also felt the need for an atonement for his sin. But sin perverts man's reason and twists his whole being. The first thing which Adam lost when he fell seems to have been his sense of good judgment, for instead of fleeing immediately to God, the only One who could possibly help him, he fled *from* God and hid himself from his Saviour and sewed fig leaves together for a covering.

### MAN'S OWN EFFORTS FRUITLESS

The fig leaves could do nothing for Adam beyond giving him a temporary employment, but left him just as guilty as he was before. And so after God had interviewed Adam and Eve and pronounced the curse upon them and all the creation, God now

147

reveals *His* plan of salvation and redemption. This we see in Genesis 3:21, a brief verse that can be easily overlooked, and yet one which is of inestimable importance and packed with information concerning the whole subsequent revelation of the Scriptures. Here it is again: "Unto Adam also and to his wife did the LORD *God make coats* of skins, and [*He*] clothed them" (Genesis 3:21).

Now study that verse in contrast to Genesis 3:7 where we are told that Adam and Eve made for themselves fig-leaf aprons in an effort to clothe their nakedness. There are many points of contrast here, but we may sum up all of them in three prominent revelations given in the verse. Adam's attempt was by his own work. God's remedy was totally and wholly and completely the work of God. Adam's efforts were without the death of the sinner, which God had said must occur. But in God's plan there was the death of a substitute, for an animal had to die before its skins could be utilized. Finally, in Adam's effort there was no shedding of blood, but in God's plan there were both the death and the shedding of the blood of an innocent victim. In these three things we have the whole plan of salvation summed up:

1. Salvation is all the work of God.
2. Salvation must be by death of a substitute.
3. Salvation must be by shedding of blood.

God Almighty Himself knows of no other plan of salvation. Unless these three requirements are met there can be no redemption from sin. This principle is revealed and laid down at the beginning of history and from there on to the last verse of Revelation there is not a hair's departure from that rule. From that day until this, and until the end of time, there has not been, nor will there be any deviation from this divinely instituted plan. From this point on, all the Scripture is but a progressive revelation of the story of *salvation by grace* as contrasted to *fig leaves* and man's efforts to save himself by his own goodness and his own works.

So we repeat, all religions fall under one of these two heads, *fig leaves* or *grace*. Man's work or God's work. Human righteousness or God's righteousness. That religion which teaches that man must do something, all or in part, to earn his salvation, was already tried by our first parents in the garden and it miserably failed. Salvation is of the Lord. The moment we add anything to grace we spoil it all. God will never share either the work or the glory for salvation with any other. Of course, when we proceed further into the Scriptures all this is made perfectly clear. Paul in writing to Titus says:

> Not by works of righteousness which we have done, but according to his mercy he saved us, by the washing of regeneration, and renewing of the Holy Ghost (Titus 3:5).

In Ephesians Paul states it just as positively:

> For by grace are ye saved through faith; and that not of yourselves: it is the gift of God:
> Not of works, lest any man should boast.
> For we are his workmanship, created in Christ Jesus unto good works, which God hath before ordained that we should walk in them (Ephesians 2:8-10).

And in Romans 4:5 we have it still stronger:

> But to him that worketh not, but believeth on him that justifieth the ungodly, his faith is counted for righteousness (Romans 4:5).

God's plan of salvation admits of no human works of any kind, not even the least bit. It must all be of grace. Man by nature is unable to do anything. Before he believes, he has no merit, no goodness, nothing to recommend him to God. "Without faith it is impossible to please God."

It may seem that we are placing undue emphasis upon this phase of the record, but I assure you that it is definitely necessary. After six thousand years of human history with God's clear revelation, there are still countless millions who have not yet learned that God prepared a finished salvation, and that redemption is the free gift of God's grace. Grace excludes all works. The moment we add the least bit of works to grace it is no more of grace, and vice versa. Paul in Romans 11:6 says:

> And if by grace, then is it no more of works: otherwise grace is no more grace. But if it be of works, then is it no more grace: otherwise work is no more work (Romans 11:6).

Notice, therefore, how terse the record in Genesis 3: "Unto Adam . . . did the LORD God make coats of skins, and [He] clothed them" (Genesis 3:21).

Can you find Adam in that picture at all? There is no mention that Adam was even present when God slew the animal and took its skins and prepared the coats for the sinner. I always have liked to believe that Adam did witness this first sacrifice, being a wonderful picture of Calvary, but there is no mention of it in the text. God did it all. God slew the animal, God devised the plan, God shed the victim's blood, God took the bloody skins, God put them upon Adam and Eve. What a picture of grace! And God's plan has not varied since. It is still the only way of salvation.

## THE THREE REQUIREMENTS

We have at various times given to you the Law of First Mention as a valuable aid in Bible study. You will recall it goes something like this: "The first time a phrase, word or event or incident occurs in the Bible, it gives the key to its meaning elsewhere in the Bible."

We have already seen that this was true of sin. Eve's first transgression was a picture of the nature and development of sin in all ages and among all men. We saw that the same thing is true of Satan. The first time he is mentioned and described in the Bible, we have the picture of his methods and approach at any other time. So, too, with fig leaves. Fig leaves we saw were man's first effort at saving himself and covering his sin, and of course he failed. Wherever else, therefore, we read of sin or Satan or fig leaves in the Bible, they always follow this pattern of the first time they are mentioned.

Now in Genesis 3:21 we have the first record in the Bible of an *acceptable sacrifice for sin*. And without an exception, this becomes the pattern for an acceptable sacrifice anywhere it occurs. Remember the three requirements. It must be *God's work;* it must be by death; it must be by the shedding of blood.

As an example of the inviolability of this rule we have but to turn to the very next chapter (Genesis 4) for an illustration of this wonderful truth. In Genesis 4 we have the first two boys ever born into the world. It is quite significant that only sinners have ever been born into the world, with one exception, *Jesus*, the God-Man. The first two people were *not born*, but created, Adam and Eve, and they soon became sinners. All children who were ever born were born sinners, but Cain and Abel had also evidently been instructed by their parents about this sacrifice of Jehovah in Genesis 3:21. We know little of their lives before Abel was murdered, but we do know that they were religious, that they knew about the necessity of a sacrifice, and also knew the inviolable rule which God had laid down in regard to the three conditions of acceptable sacrifice. You will recall that Cain was the more religious of the two, but was lost and became a murderer. He was a farmer and was the first one to think of the need of acknowledging God, and he brought a sacrifice of the fruits of the field, but he was rejected. Abel, on the other hand, brought a firstling of the flock, a little lamb, and slew it, poured out its blood and was accepted of the Lord.

There is nothing in the record to show that Cain was not sincere or that he did not bring a beautiful and expensive sacrifice, and yet God would not accept it. And why? Because it was only a repetition of his parents' fig-leaf religion. Cain ignored God's rule, that an acceptable sacrifice must be all of the Lord, must be by death, and must be by blood. Instead he brought of the labor of his own hands, the fruit of the field. There was no death involved, and no blood shed.

Now contrast with this the offering of faithful Abel. Up to the point of sacrifice there is no difference apparent in these two boys. They were both religious, they both felt their responsibility to God, they both acted upon that feeling and brought something to God, but with entirely different results. In Hebrews 11 we have the key to the answer. *"By faith Abel offered unto God a more excellent sacrifice than Cain"* (Hebrews 11:4). By *faith!* By *faith!* Faith in what? Faith in the Word of God as recorded in Genesis 3:21. He believed God's Word in regard to the three requirements of salvation, and so he met these requirements and brought a lamb. See how all three of God's provisions are met:

1. The lamb was God's gift of creation; not his own labor.
2. The lamb was put to death as a substitute.
3. The blood was shed.

And God looked upon that offering of *faith* and Abel is today in Heaven, and Cain is in Hell. Not because Cain was not as religious, or as good morally, or that he did not bring as nice a sacrifice, but all because he *did not believe God* in regard to the only way of salvation. *Fig leaves! Fig leaves!* Over and over again. Trace this throughout the Scriptures. See Noah's sacrifice of animals after the flood. They were God's provision, for He had commanded Noah to take *seven* of the clean animals, instead of the *two* of all others. Suppose God had not commanded *seven* of the clean animals; there would have been no substitute to offer, no blood. But God provided for that blood by His forethought and provision for the additional clean animals. It was God's gift, it was by death, and it was by blood. Trace it in the Passover, through all the offerings of the Old Testament, until the type becomes reality when God's Lamb came into the world nineteen hundred years ago, to die and to shed His blood that we might be saved. And did this Lamb, Jesus, fulfill the requirements laid down in Genesis 3:21? Listen:

1. He was God's gift — "For God so loved the world, that he gave his only begotten Son . . ." (John 3:16).
2. It was by the death of a substitute — "Who his own self bare our sins in his own body on the tree, that we, being dead to sins, should live unto righteousness" (I Peter 2:24).
3. And it was by blood — "The blood of Jesus Christ his Son cleanseth us from all sin" (I John 1:7).

Ah, my friend, see at what cost your salvation was purchased. See to what lengths the Lord has gone to make this simple plan of salvation clear that none might be kept in ignorance of His only way of salvation. Why then cling to your fig leaves or your own righteousness and good works? Why then trust in anything else but His Word?

> Believe on the Lord Jesus Christ, and thou shalt be saved . . . (Acts 16:31).